PRO SE PRISONER:
GUIDE TO BUILD WEALTH

Cryptocurrency, Real Estate & Business

C.A. Knuckles

Freebird Publishers

221 Pearl St., Ste. 541, North Dighton, MA 02764

Info@FreebirdPublishers.com

www.FreebirdPublishers.com

All Freebird Publishers titles, imprints, and distributed lines are available at special quantity discounts for bulk purchases for sales promotions, premiums, fundraising, educational, or institutional use.

ISBN: 978-1-952159-47-3

Printed in the United States of America

DEDICATION

To those lost in the cycle of poverty, incarceration, and poverty-stricken ghettos. Behind me is a strong woman who has pushed me to do great things. I will never forget the role you played in my success. I love you, and thank you!

.

ACKNOWLEDGEMENT

Thanks to Freebird Publishers for their support. I want to extend my appreciation to all the people who helped with research for this book series. I am grateful to all the prisoners who became pro se prisoners by purchasing my books in the Pro Se Prisoners: Guide to Build Wealth series. I sincerely thank you for your continued support, and I will keep providing knowledge.

Thank you. The Forgotten Voices!

CONTENTS

KEYS TO CREATING GENERATIONAL WEALTH

We have to break generational curses that prevent our upward mobility from creating wealth. Inside most of the communities we come from, we have a school-to-prison pipeline that has devastated our neighborhoods.

Where I'm at, Maryland has the highest incarceration rate for black people in the U.S.A. per the "Sentencing Project". Maryland has a 30% black population, yet blacks make up 71% of its prison population. These are generational problems that started before you and will stop because of you.

Our goal is to create generational wealth based on financial knowledge put into action. It's not money but knowledge that makes you rich. All the money principles that you learned from your parents and grandparents continue to make you poor because they were taught poor financial practices. It's on you not to teach your kids a poverty mindset. To build wealth and create generational wealth, you need a vast amount of knowledge of how money works. Once you know how money works, it becomes an asset that is more valuable than physical money because it allows you to make it appear out of thin air, just like banks do. One of the generational curses in the poverty system is "welfare," which has created more poor people in a system that's already on the verge of collapse.

Creating generational wealth for the future generations of your family and community is the pillar of breaking down this current system. Let's get a few things out of the way first. Just know that 70% of families lose wealth by the second generation. 90% of wealthy families lose all their wealth by the third generation. Stop reading headlines that paint this rose-studded picture of wealthy families and pick one to blame and say they have generational wealth passed down from generations before them. That's the news clip, that's the Forbes Magazine article. Look at the numbers above: in the 2nd generation, 70% lose their wealth, and in the 3rd generation, 90% lose it. It's rare to do, but my focus is on something else inside the generational wealth-building system in the U.S.A. It's not about families creating generational wealth; to me, the focus should be on the "financial system" designed for a few and not the many. If these systems weren't in place, none of this would be possible. So, it's the system of wealth and its many vehicles that drive the creation of long-term capital for the wealthy.

Personal Wealth vs. Family Wealth

$100,000 in bank account is personal wealth. Thus, it can be depleted.	Liquid hard to change. Less likely to blow through money/assets.

Our goal is to build family wealth or turn personal wealth into family wealth. Another strategy that can be utilized is using "Holding Companies". The wealth that is passed down from one generation to the next is considered generational wealth. Starting a "Holding Company" provides this by doing this:

1. "Holding Company" that owns 100% of your LLC [Set-Up Trust]
2. Make yourself the trustee and your family the beneficiary.
3. Spend all the money on them, and what's left over, you donate to the family foundation that you will also set up.
4. Make your family foundation private and apply for [501c3].

These are all vehicles to store wealth tax-free for generations to come. Remember, the IRS taxes income. What we are doing is turning income that would otherwise be taxed into tax-free money!

Quick Tips on How to Build Generational Wealth

1. Invest in your child's education
   Teach your kids early on about personal finances and financial literacy.
2. Long-term stock market investing

   Invest in index funds for the long term. Set aside money every week to invest in the [S&P 500 Index Fund], which has annual returns of 5%- 7%.
3. Real Estate Investing

   Rental property ownership creates income. Using 1031 exchanges makes it tax-free. Using other people's money [credit cards/bank loans/refinancing] is key.
4. Create a business
5. Buy artwork
6. Buy land
7. Life Insurance [cash-value]

Passing It Down

1. Write a will
   Instructions on what to do with your assets.

2. Set up trust.

   Legal entity to hold and transfer assets.

3. Name beneficiaries

   Choose who gets your assets. Plan wisely!

4. Don't miss a step in the process; you will be taxed, and nobody will get your assets.

So, the moral of the story is to build your own table now so your kids and community don't ever have to ask for a place at someone else's table.

According to Cerulli Associates, over the next 25 years, $68 trillion will transfer from U.S. households to heirs and charities. Make sure to be a part of that transfer and stake your claim.

Pro Se Prisoner

C.A. Knuckles

CRYPTOCURRENCY INVESTING FOR WEALTH

WHAT IS CRYPTOCURRENCY

Cryptocurrency is decentralized digital money that's based on blockchain technology. It works as a digital encrypted and decentralized medium of exchange. Unlike Fiat currency [i.e., U.S. Dollar], no central authority manages a cryptocurrency's value. Goods and services can be bought with cryptocurrencies, plus you can invest in other assets like stocks, etc.

Blockchain is an open, distributed ledger that records transactions in code. Think of it as a checkbook that's distributed across multiple computers around the world. All transactions are recorded in "blocks" that link together on a chain of previous cryptocurrency transactions. There are multiple ways to purchase and/or buy cryptocurrency, but most use exchanges such as Coinbase, Kraken, Gemini, Robinhood, Webull, eToro, Crypto.com, Uphold, Public, and Plynkinvest.com, etc. Most require no minimum of $0.00 and have no fees associated with trading. Usually, you can invest for as little as $1.00. Also, check out my previous book about Crypto: "Pro se Prisoner: How To Buy Stocks and Bitcoin" by C.A. Knuckles. Available for purchase through Amazon.com or FreebirdPublishers.com.

TOP 25 Cryptocurrency

Bitcoin [BTC]	$69,175.41
Ethereum [ETH]	$3,422.36
Tether [USDT]	$0.9998
USD Coin [USDC]	$0.9999
BNB [BNB]	$578.80
XRP [XRP]	$0.5902
Cardano [ADA]	$0.5844
Solana [SOL]	$176.71
Polkadot [DOT]	$8.60
Dogecoin [DOGE]	$0.1962
Polygon [MATIC]	$0.8968
Shiba Inu [SHIB]	$0.00002786

Dai [DAI]	$0.9998
Avalanche [AVAX]	$48.56
Litecoin [LTC]	$100.34
Cronus [CRO]	$0.1443
Stellar [XLM]	$0.128
Terra Classic [LUNC]	$0.0001316
Bitcoin Cash	$694.55
Algorand [ALGO]	$0.2329
EOS [EOS]	$1.01
ApeCoin	$1.68
Tezos [XTZ]	$1.25
Axie Infinity	$9.64
Terra [Luna]	$0.8851

Cryptocurrency to Buy Now

1. Bitcoin [BTC]
2. Ethereum [ETH]
3. Mirror [MIR]
4. Helium [HNT]
5. Swerve [SWRV]
6. Saddle Finance [SDL]
7. Luna Inu [LINU]
8. Arc [ARC]
9. Ridotto [RDT]
10. Ravencoin [RVN]

Other Cryptocurrency Options to Invest

Investing through exchanges is one way to get exposure to cryptocurrency. We spoke about SDIRAs in the second part of book one, "*Pro se Prisoner Guide to Build Wealth: Credit & Taxes*", but I also waited until this part to tell you about investing in Bitcoin with your SDIRA. Bitcoin IRA allows you to invest, buy, and sell 60+ cryptocurrencies in your SDIRA account. Using Bitcoinira.com, you can invest tax-free in Bitcoin and other cryptocurrencies. 24/7, you can buy and sell cryptocurrencies using this platform.

While SDIRAs are one way to invest, another way is Cryptocurrency ETFs, which are funds that consist of cryptocurrencies but trade on the open market. Cryptocurrency ETFs are different from traditional ETFs that track an "Index"; crypto ETFs track the price of one or more digital tokens, such as Bitcoin. There are only two types of Cryptocurrency ETFs. 1) is backed by physical cryptocurrencies, and 2) is a synthetic variant that tracks cryptocurrency derivatives like futures contracts and cryptocurrency exchange-traded products [ETPs]. Top cryptocurrency ETFs are:

- Amplify Transformational Data Sharing ETF [BLOK]
- Bitwise 10 Crypto Index Fund [BITW]
- Siren NASDAQ NexGen Economy ETR [BLCN]
- First Trust Indxx Innovative Transaction and Process ETF [LEGR]
- Bitwise Crypto Industry Innovators ETF [BITQ]
- Global X Blockchain ETF [BKCH]
- Global X Blockchain & Bitcoin Strategy EFT [BITS]
- Grayscale Bitcoin Trust [GBTC]
- First Trust Skybridge Crypto Industry and Digital Economy ETF [CRPT]
- VanEck Digital Transformation ETF [DAPP]
- Fidelity Crypto Industry and Digital Payments ETF [FDIG]
- Capital Link Global Fintech [KOIN]

ETFs are available for investment, but you can also invest directly in the companies that make money in this area, such as:

- Coinbase Global, Inc. [COIN]
- Tesla, Inc [TSLA]
- NVIDIA Corporation [NVDA]
- Advanced Micro Devices, Inc. [AMD]
- Block [SQ]
- Pay-Pal Holdings [PYPL]
- Marathon Digital Holdings, Inc [MARA]
- Riot Blockchain, Inc [RIOT]
- MicroStrategy, Inc. [MSTR]
- CME Group, Inc. [CME]
- Hut 8 Mining Corp. [HUT]

Don't shy away from crypto investing because of volatility; more and more companies have taken an interest in this Technology of the future, so don't miss out. Crypto mining companies allow you to invest in the process of mining crypto without actually buying mining equipment and rigs to do it yourself. These crypto-mining companies use computers to solve complex computational problems, validate blockchain transactions, and generate new cryptocurrency coins. It's also costly to mine crypto yourself but also sporadically rewarding. All cryptocurrency needs miners to perform complex computational work to verify transactions. Instead of worrying or doing things yourself, invest in some of these crypto stocks that mine crypto.

Some of the TOP stocks in this space are:

- Argo Blockchain [ARBK]
- Canaan, Inc. [CAN]
- Hive Blockchain Technologies, Ltd. [HIVE]
- Stronghold Digital Mining [SDIG]
- Bit Digital [BTBT]
- Core Scientific, Inc. [CORE]
- Bitfarms Ltd. [BITF]
- Riot Blockchain, Inc. [RIOT]
- Marathon Digital Holdings [MARA]
- Clean Spark, Inc. [CLSK]

Pro se Tip: (!)

4 Major Types of Crypto

1. Utility
2. Payment
3. Security
4. Stablecoin

THE METAVERSE 101

The Metaverse has been described by many as the future of the internet. Metaverse and blockchain are what many people also say is "web 3.0". We are in the middle of building out a new form of technology, communication, and the internet. This space is not just one specific type of technology but rather a broad shift in how we interact with technology. Sitting in prison might seem like you shouldn't know about the Metaverse, but it's too important of an investment not to mention it here. Currently, big and small companies are building virtual reality settings. Within that virtual reality, you can act out your wildest fantasy or buy virtual real estate using cryptocurrency, which you would own. This new digital economy will allow you to create, buy, and sell goods like in the real world. Even Meta is now the name of Facebook's parent company. Some forms of the Metaverse are already here, like MMOs that are entire virtual worlds, digital concerts, video calls that connect people worldwide, online avatars, and commerce platforms [Hence Roblox]. A new complex world awaits exploring, and only this one is digital.

These Metaverse networks are vast networks where you can use avatars to interact socially. They let you go beyond just viewing digital content and immersing you in spaces where the physical and digital worlds converge. How would you invest in this market of the future? One way is to purchase and invest in cryptocurrency; you could also invest in companies; thirdly, you could put your money in ETFs that focus on gaming, blockchain, and the Metaverse itself.

Companies that have Metaverse potential are:

- Meta [owns Facebook, Instagram, etc.]
- Microsoft [Just acquired Activision Blizzard for Metaverse]
- Cassava Sciences, Inc.
- Anavex Life Sciences
- Nvidia [NVDA]
- Tesla
- Sea Limited ADR
- Match Group [MTCH]
- Unity Software, Inc. [U]
- Matterport, Inc. [MTTR]
- Roblox Corp. [RBLX]

- Autodesk [ADSK]

Some Metaverse ETFs that invest in the broad Metaverse market are:
- The Metaverse ETF [METV]
- Evolve Metaverse ETF [MESH]
- Horizons Global Metaverse Index ETF [MTAV]
- The Simplify Volt Web3 ETF [WIII]
- 21 Shares Decentralized ETF [MANA]
- Global X FinTech ETF [FINX]
- Pro Shares Ultra Pro QQQ [TQQQ]
- SPDR S&P Software and Services ETF [XSW]
- Vanguard Information Technology Index Fund ETF Shares [VGI]
- Fidelity MCSI Information Technology Index ETF [FTEC]

Right now, the Metaverse is new and still evolving. The perfect time to invest is now, not when these companies or tech blow up. Making your money now will create a major income stream for you. Immerse yourself in the Metaverse and build wealth.

NFTs [NON-FUNGIBLE TOKEN]

These are records on the blockchain associated with a digital asset. How this works is, that ownership is placed on the Blockchain but can be easily transferred to another person, thus allowing NFTs to be sold and traded instantly. While these assets have been typically associated with Art, NFTs can refer to digital files such as photos, videos, and audio. NFTs are assets, hence why they are non-fungible, unlike fungible cryptocurrencies. People are so hyped up about NFTs because they provide public certificates of authenticity or proof of ownership. The growth of NFTs has taken off in recent years. Non-fungible means it's unique and can't be replaced with something else. As I spoke about cryptocurrency being fungible, you will have the same thing if you trade one for another similar cryptocurrency. Non-fungible NFTs are one of a kind; if traded, you will have something completely different.

NFTs work as a part of the Ethereum blockchain. Ethereum is a cryptocurrency like Bitcoin, but its blockchain supports NFTs. While NFTs can be anything digital you create, the craze has been excitement around using tech to sell digital art.

Popular NFT collections and communities include "Pudgy Penguins" and the "Crypto Punks" community, but the most famous is the animal-themed "Bored Ape Yacht Club". The former and latter have vast communities that talk and share images on places like the Discord app. The advantage of NFTs for the average person depends on the purpose. If you are an artist in this space [If you draw in prison, this could be a new stream of income], NFTs give you a way to sell your artwork to a broader audience with a bigger market. The bonus is that NFTs allow you to get paid a percentage every time the NFT is sold or changes hands. Unlike a physical picture drawn on paper, once purchased, there's no royalty after the buyer sells it. But NFTs allow you to enable a feature that lets you profit every time someone resells your artwork.

If you would rather buy NFTs, the best advantage is that you get basic usage rights, like being able to post online. Many mainstream people and companies, such as Marvel, are creating and selling their own NFTs. Companies like NIKE have recently patented a method to verify sneakers' authenticity using an NFT system. With the call "Cryptokicks." Remember, the term "NFT" only gained this wide use you see now because of the "ERC-721" standard that was put up on Ethereum GitHub. Now, all industries are being impacted by this potential multi-billion-dollar sector. From music, film, and art, NFTs have pushed these sectors forward. Some problems exist that are now being addressed, such as copyright issues associated with the double selling of images and downloading free copies of original art or images. Also, it's been hard to enforce copyrights because of how the blockchain is set up to be decentralized. These platforms have to be the ones that stop the double duplication of people's art, etc.

How To Invest in NFTs

STEP 1

Choose an NFT you like:

a piece of art, music, or

an item within a video game

STEP 2

Find out which type of

crypto is needed to buy

your targeted NFT

STEP 3

Open and fund a crypto

wallet on the marketplace

STEP 4

You can buy an NFT at a

fixed price or via a virtual

auction. Buy your NFT or place

a bid and wait to see if you get

the NFT you chose.

Other steps include purchasing Ethereum on a cryptocurrency exchange [such as Coinbase, Robinhood, Binance, etc.], transferring crypto to the crypto wallet, then connecting the wallet to the NFT marketplace and buying your chosen NFT.

Several marketplaces exist that make the purchase of NFTs more accessible, such as:

- Async Art [www.async.art]
- Axie Marketplace
- Crypto.com
- Dencentraland.org

- Foundation.app
- OpenSea.io
- Rarible.com
- Sorare.com
- Superrare.com
- Axieinfinity.com
- Knownorigin.io
- Lookrare.org
- Magiceden.io
- Mintable.app
- NBATOPshop.com
- NiftyGateway.com
- Marketplacedraftkings.com

Resources on top NFTs: www.bestnftplatforms.io. The NFT market is wide open for investment, whether you want to buy, sell, or create your own NFTs. Looking at the future, NFTs combined with the Metaverse will create a whole new class of assets of the future.

ICO [INITIAL COIN OFFERING]

ICOs are another cryptocurrency investment that is used differently than other forms discussed previously. It's a type of funding using cryptocurrencies, more like regular crowdfunding projects. Furthermore, the process involves selling cryptocurrency in the form of "tokens", to potential investors and/or speculators alike. These tokens will turn into functional units of currency if the ICO meets its funding goals or if the project underpinning the project has a successful launch. What's important to note is that ICOs are a source of capital for start-ups and can be a vehicle to avoid tough regulations about seeking investments from the public directly. A little history is in order for ICOs. The first token sale was held by Mastercoin in 2013, and Ethereum had a token sale in 2014. But until 2017, 4 years later, tokens and I.C.O.s caught fire. Multiple websites appeared: web browser Brave raised millions, the messaging app Kik raised $100 million, and ICO sales peaked at 2.3 billion. Filecoin raised $257 million in 2018, and ICOs took off. From this, multiple scams arose, such as pumping and disposing of coins, and regulations were slim to none.

All that said, good I.C.O.s still exist to invest in and around the world. At www.icodrops.com, there is a calendar of active and upcoming ICOs and IEOs [Initial Exchange Offerings]. At the same time, you can also look at www.coinmarketcap.com/ico-calendar to get the latest ICOs to invest in. Once you check the above sites, one more thing to do when you use the CoinMarketCap website is to make sure to type "All best ICOs" in the search bar to get the best results. Pick a platform to purchase, and find a crypto wallet such as Ledger, Binance, or Coinbase. There are also Web 3 wallets like MetaMask and Trust Wallet, which are better because they are more frequently used for ICO purchases. Acquire the "native token" of the ICO to pay transaction fees. Move the token to a popular Web3 Wallet [MetaMask], then go to the ICO website and connect your wallet. Purchase ICO but keep some tokens in your wallet for transaction fees. You then will claim tokens from ICO. If you want to make some return on your investment right away, then sell your newly acquired token on [Dex], which is a decentralized peer-to-peer exchange where people can trade cryptocurrency directly without a middleman.

This form of venture capital that funds projects using tokens with direct access to anybody in the world is the future of start-up funding. ICOs put the power back in the hands of the people. Why is this so important? Until very recently, the average investor only had one chance to invest in an IPO, and that was when they began trading on the stock exchange. By that time, those initial investors [venture capitalists, banks, etc.] had already put money in before the IPO, which means that once it went public, they made boatloads of money. IPOs were something only the wealthy could invest in.

All that changed with ICOs and 2012 with the jump start of our business startups [JOBS Act]. It provided equity-based opportunities to nonaccredited investors [average citizens]. With this, ICOs were a part of regulation for the first time and had been legitimized by the government. The JOBS Act regulation issued rules about creating and implementing portals for investment opportunities. In 80 years of only allowing the wealthy accredited investors to be the only ones who gain access and wealth through IPOs [Initial Public Offerings] of shares of publicly traded companies, the JOBS Act, for the first time, allowed nonaccredited investors gateways to invest in private startups and receive compensation in the form of Equity. Crypto Assets and ICO protocol must be directly monetized directly for the application to work. ICOs have to make money or be created to make money for it to be placed on the blockchain network. To have value, applications like ICOs must store value, thus creating a vast opportunity for growth for nonaccredited investors that is greater than any other form of venture capital funding. Remember, Initial Coin Offerings describes a form of crowdfunding to fund a new crypto asset. New ICOs always pop up, so do your homework on the ICOs before investing. Websites like [www.smithandcrown.com] are great sources of information. It gives you current, past, and upcoming ICO sales. Then there is [www.icocountdown.com] and [www.cyber.fund].

Opportunities will grow as this space continues to be successful and information to the public is shaped in a new way so more average citizens can invest in these alternative means. Taking back your financial well-being is important. Right now, as you sit in prison making financial decisions, create goals and objectives you want to meet in this space. New laws like the JOBS Act provide chances for future success and new investment venues.

Some of the best ICO cryptos for 2022 to look into are:

- Lucky Block
- Lixiana
- Visa MetaFi
- Chain of Legends
- Subquery
- Koakuma
- PixelHub
- Fusca
- Juniverse Token
- Bioviratech

ICOs open the door for you to build wealth by financing startups from their inception. Thus, equity-based opportunities are provided to the average citizen, who is usually left out of venture capital and early-stage investment opportunities.

BITCOIN

Upgrade Bitcoin Rewards

New ways to use Bitcoin are developed by tech companies every day. Upgrade is another example of expanding areas for Bitcoin to thrive. They are a financial technology company that offers affordable and responsible credit to mainstream consumers through cards and personal loans. Plus, with the added bonus of credit monitoring, you completely control your financial well-being. Benefits include:

- Unlimited 1.5% back in Bitcoin when you make payments.
- No Fees
- Credit Lines from $500 to $25,000
- Used wherever Visa is accepted
- Pay down balances from each month at a fixed rate with equal monthly payments
- Assuming $10,000 balance; 2 years to pay off with $2,102.71 interest paid over a period of time
- Bitcoin Rewards Card, where you get rewarded with Bitcoin

Another way to build wealth using cryptocurrency is by applying to this Bitcoin Rewards program offered by Upgrade.com.

Cash App Bitcoin Investing

No one in prison or outside of prison doesn't know about Cash App services. The main reason for this service is to make it easier to send money without going through a traditional Western Union service. But the real value to me isn't the process of money in seconds but the ability to allow anyone with an account to invest as little as $1.00 into Bitcoin, stocks, and ETFs. Easy and simple steps to achieve this are simple:

- Download the Cash App [If your outside network has one, use that
- Go to the investing tab with the Bitcoin logo
- Input the amount you want to invest; you will own that % of whatever Bitcoin is trading when you purchase it.

Easy, simple, and to the point! Get started now with building wealth through cryptocurrency.

Top 7 Bitcoin Wallets

Quickly, here are some of the best crypto wallets that can be used to transfer crypto such as Bitcoin, with others or off exchanges.

- Trust Wallet
- Coinbase Wallet
- Exodus Crypto Wallet
- Meta Mask – Best for Ethereum
- Blue Wallet – Best for defi wallet
- Mycelium – Best for mobile devices

Many more wallets exist, but these are the top ones that get the most done for you. Get your network to check them out; some are apps that can be easily downloaded, and some have websites.

TOP CRYPTOCURRENCY EXCHANGES

These exchanges offer access to the 1,000 cryptocurrencies on the open market and offer multiple types of cryptocurrency to buy, sell, and trade.

- Coinbase App
- Robinhood App
- Binance.us
- Etoro.com
- Cash App
- Changelly.com
- Crypto.com
- Bisq-network
- Sofi.com
- Gemini App
- Kraken.com
- Uphold.com
- Bitmart.com
- Public.com
- Webull.com

Use your network to get these accounts set up and begin the process of investing, selling, and trading crypto currency to build wealth also, if you haven't already ordered my first book to get a more in-depth look into crypto investing. Order from the #1 inmate publisher of prisoner publications: Freebird Publishers, www.freebirdpublishers.com.

"Pro se Prisoner: How to Buy Stocks and Bitcoin" by C.A. Knuckles

REAL ESTATE INVESTING FOR WEALTH

REAL ESTATE EXPLAINED

For many of us, real estate is a house to live in. Most of us also grew up living in Section B housing without ever owning real estate. This limited understanding of real estate has left us out of the wealth conversation. We can't talk about real estate without talking about "Homeowner's Loan Corporation." The U.S. Government created this corporation to lend money during the Great Depression to prevent home foreclosures. This program excluded black people, thus the government-sponsored "Redlining," where the U.S.A. government drew lines in colors around neighborhoods in which black people were "red," meaning banks couldn't lend to them. The greatest wealth-building asset at the time was home equity, for which blacks were excluded, lost homes, and became ghettos and poverty-stricken slums run by government assistance and Section 8 housing. [More on this later.]

Starting our journey through real estate, we must also address or explain the multiple types of real estate. What is real estate?

#1 Residential: This means single-family homes, duplexes, and townhouses.

#2 Commercial: These include office buildings, gas stations, and shopping centers.

#3 Industrial: These include factories, power plants, and warehouses.

All these groups of real estate are investment opportunities to build wealth. These big income-producing assets come with massive tax breaks, deductions, and sometimes no taxes. When we speak about residential real estate, know that in order to build wealth by using real estate, it must be based on income-producing real estate that you are able to build a business from by using rent to gain continued income. It's a liability to buy a single-family residence just to live in! So that means even buying a personal residence to live in is a liability. Here's why: Houses were created for banks to profit, not for people to profit. The banks lend out money for you to buy the house, and you pay the loan back and rent to someone else every month. The wealthy do this instead: They get the loan through an LLC they own, buy the house, pay rent to the LLC every month, and the LLC gets tax deductions, appreciation, etc. Always think about tax-free business structures because, as you will see in this part, I will show you how to use a 1031 exchange and never pay taxes until you want! Buying real estate using an LLC and collecting income from rent is a protection against high inflation. But the greatest tool you have at your side is (O.P.M.= Other People's Money), which will help you buy rental properties and let it pay for itself through rent collected from your tenants. As stated earlier, there are amazing benefits to building wealth this way, such as cash flow, tax benefits, appreciation, depreciation, and benefits of use.

Pro se Tip: (!)

You can't expect to grow and also stay the same. Choose your mindset. Poverty or Wealthy. Your choice!

Another thing is, don't just sit in your cell and think this is too good to be true, or you start questioning if you can achieve success because you can! With negative thoughts going through your mind, you must ignore them and don't let your environment—in prison or out–add to it. All you have to do is start believing you can get out and take the next step, which is action.

Pro se Tip: (!)

72% of whites are homeowners. While just 42% of blacks are.

Quick note: I was reading about wealth in some papers I had, and I wrote something down two years ago by Scott Galloway (Prof. G.) in which he broke down "The Algebra of Wealth":

Wealth = Focus + (Stoicism x Time x Diversification)

Something that simply explains wealth building to a "T." Before we move on to the next section, always remember to never focus on real estate investing alone. Don't be a one-trick-pony because real estate has created 90% of millionaires. And it's the single least way people become billionaires! Why? Real estate has price compression, meaning anybody can invest; hence, 90% of millionaires are able to do so. We want to become billionaires; that's the Pro se Prisoner mindset. The one category that has created more billionaires is "Private Equity"; these investors buy deals off the market. Looking back at the "Algebra of Wealth," a key to that formula is (X Diversification); we must check all the equity and asset boxes and never think that the key to wealth is real estate alone because it's not. It's just a piece of the wealth-building puzzle.

STRUCTURING LLC TO BUY REAL ESTATE

Real estate is an effective way to start your wealth-building journey. Having an LLC and buying real estate with an LLC is the best structure you can get. This means your company will operate as the landlord, not you as an individual, and it offers major tax benefits and protections.

Setting up the LLC should be easy. There are many ways to do it quickly and easily. As previously provided in the "Business Wealth Section," you can do it yourself by contacting your state's Secretary of State, obtaining your E.I.N. number, setting up a business bank account, and writing an operating agreement (check the Business Building Section for expanded details). Once the above is completed, go back to book one, "Pro se Prisoner's Guide to Build Wealth: Credit and Taxes," and follow the steps to build your business credit. After you've built up about 90-120 days of building credit, go to the bank where your account has been set up and get a mortgage loan under your new LLC name. There are conventional mortgage loans and portfolio loans, which the lender keeps in-house and doesn't report the mortgage on your credit report. There is no limit to the number of properties you can buy, plus it is cheaper, faster, and more flexible. Others include "Purchase-Rehab Loans": these come from hard money lenders; while it's a short-term loan, it's still good to get first, then get a long-term loan after, with the added bonus of refinancing and using that money on top of the loan, to expand your real estate holdings.

Pro se Tip: (!)
Financing: Cash, equity, debt (bank/land contracts).

Structuring your LLC to be in the real estate arena is important for two reasons: protection/liability and tax benefits and wealth creation through passive income. The diagram below shows what protection looks like.

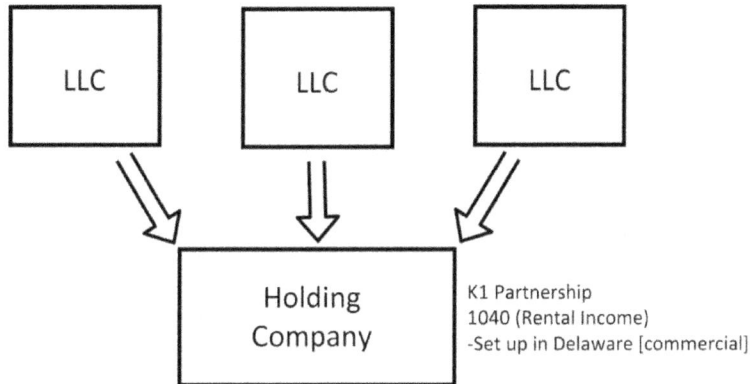

```
┌─────────┐    ┌─────────┐    ┌─────────┐
│   LLC   │    │   LLC   │    │   LLC   │
└─────────┘    └─────────┘    └─────────┘
      ↓              ↓              ↓
     ┌──────────────────────────┐
     │       Holding            │    K1 Partnership
     │       Company            │    1040 (Rental Income)
     │                          │    -Set up in Delaware [commercial]
     └──────────────────────────┘
```

The above shows how to structure your real estate for protection properly. First, the LLCs will be established in whatever state you plan to buy real estate in. Each rental property will be placed in a different LLC, and each LLC will enter into a partnership with your holding company, which will be set up in a state (Like Wyoming) for residential rental property, etc. However, if you are buying commercial real estate, set up a company in Delaware; it offers greater protection for commercial real estate. The purpose of the Partnership with the holding company is for tax purposes because you want (rental income) to come in as a K1 Partnership and get K1 on (1040 form) (see example in index). You also must understand that setting up your company in Wyoming offers anonymity because you don't have to list who manages it or who the members are (greater protection).

Another thing is that where the property is will determine how to structure your LLC, for example:

> FL: Uses Land Trust
>
> PA: Unrecorded DEED into LLC
>
> CA: Statutory Trust (WY) (W.S.T.)
>
> OH & TX: Series LLC

When to form a structure will also depend on the property you invest in. Commercial Property: Five units or better, the structure needs to be set up before buying real estate (LLC). It is the same thing with residential setup upfront; make an offer in the LLC name and close in the LLC name. When trying to get a lender to loan money it's best to setup upfront when dealing with Portfolio Lender, because you want to make offers on terms in your LLC. With a Traditional Lender, you can set up later. This is the case when dealing with Fannie Mae and Freddie Mac.

Pro se Tip: (!)

Avoid personal liability placing deed and title to property in the LLC. Name online the LLC name, only the LLC (and not you) would be named as a defendant if someone is injured at your property.

Getting a loan and taking on debt is a powerful concept for real estate if you know how to use it.

Remember, since 1971, all money has been in debt, and most of all trades have been in debt. Real estate debt is the best debt because of all of the loopholes, and debt is tax-free. That's why refinancing is a powerful tool to buy more tax-free assets. Okay, you're thinking DEBT? For real? Yes, even though:

> Consumer Debt: Is $14.9 Trillion
>
> Household Debt: Is $5,315
>
> US GDP: $21 Trillion

You will build wealth with assets much faster once you learn how to use it in real estate. Structuring an LLC for real estate is about asset protection. Asset protection is all about strategy; one must plan to prevail and succeed in this area.

Also, a part of that planning should be how best to utilize loans/debt and other people's money to make proper investments in real estate. One of the best processes to do this is as follows:

🏠 = $250K ⇒ bank to get mortgage ⇒ value raises the house ⇒ rent out to cover mortgage, insurance ⇒ 🏠 bank to refinance house/mortgage ⇒ 80% mortgage ⇒ $280K ⇒ 200K to cover first mortgage ⇒ rinse repeat above. This creates multiple assets with multiple streams of income, just off using debt, which is tax-free.

Another step is "BRRRR" investing, and you do this by doing the following steps:

Buy | Buy | Rehab | Rehab | Rent | Rent | Refinance | 1st house | 2nd house | Repeat

Simple pictures, no explanation needed; this process never stops. It's the easy way to build wealth repeatedly using real estate.

Another way to start out is by investing in income-producing single-family homes with occupied tenants who pay consistently. With a $100,000 dollar price tag, you can get a loan with 20% down. Then, move on to buying multi-family properties, where you are doubling your monthly income from multiple tenants. Remember, get financing in place before the deal. Owner-occupied is more likely to receive a bank loan and a lower interest rate. This is because it is less risky for banks who lend the money. These kinds of properties with bank loans are also eligible for securitization from Fannie Mae and Freddie Mac. You can also apply for [504 loans] from the Small Business Administration, which offers loans for fixed assets [e.g., real estate, buildings, machinery, etc.] [More on loans later].

Pro se Tip: (!)

LEVERAGE: Ratio of debt (i.e. the amount that is loaned to you) to value of the asset. When you borrow money for an investment, you must receive more in profits than the interest you owe in order for the investment to be profitable.

One of the main benefits of buying real estate is that an LLC provides protection, where profits from properties aren't taxed directly; instead, they report profits on their personal tax returns.

Defined as pass-through taxation, the LLC benefits should be counted correctly. It gets even better when you purchase a home with money borrowed from a bank as a down payment. Buying real estate through an LLC and then borrowing against it means the debt is tax-free. Having real estate gives you the opportunity to shelter cash flow from real estate but also offsets other income from taxes.

Structuring your business to buy real estate is about benefiting from all the available options. Not just asset protection but taxes and tax-free loans. You get a tax-free loan, and you get to keep your assets by knowing how to refinance. Again tax-free! Here are some websites and Apps that your family can research and copy some real estate listings:

- Zillow.com or [App]
- Realtor.com
- Trulia [App]
- Roofstock.com

City-owned real estate can be found on your local city or county government website. Look under the Housing Development section.

HISTORY OF REDLINING

Real estate wealth building can't be discussed without us shedding some light on the history of redlining. While the "New Deal" was economic relief for some in 1933, the HOLL [Homeowners Loan Corporation] was established to help existing homeowners who were in default on mortgages because of the "Great Depression". Several programs were established through the New Deal, which was supposed to establish a government-backed mortgage system. HOLCs intent was to stabilize the nation's mortgage system. The process was to buy mortgages that were in default and provide better terms to struggling citizens. But what took place was a devastating practice that conditioned access to federally backed home loans on the perceived economic health of a neighborhood and used demographic factors such as race. The term they called this was "Redlining," designed by and drawn up by HOLC in the 1930s, which segregated neighborhoods with a color-coded map, using "red" to denote and show areas that were perceived to be "hazards" for lending. These effects reached beyond lending and into access to credit, where people could live, thus determining de facto where families sent their kids to public school. These deemed "hazardous" areas were zoned to underperforming schools. For 30-plus years, some form of this was legal, but in the 1960s and 1970, congress reversed actions taken by government officials in the 1930s; the problem still exists and has set back education in these areas. The red zones from the 1930s still house the same citizens. So, for generations, this effect controlled a real estate system that was supposed to be reversed and banned by the Government. Right now, the correlation between neighborhood income and redlining shows neighborhoods rated by HOLC as green or best in the 1930s are high-income neighborhoods today; none have been deemed low-income by any metrics. More than half of neighborhoods rated "Hazardous" or "Red areas" are low-income now and were the same back then. These red-lining neighborhoods continue to be the worst economic mobility neighborhoods. Today, 63% of the "hazardous" or "red" areas are still majority-minority. HOLC, or The Homeowners Loan Corporation, was created as a lending program to prevent home foreclosures during The Great Depression. This program excluded black people. Another area of this redlining system that people never include in any discussion about redlining is the fact that there is a correlation between neighborhoods that were redlined and neighborhoods that have a high density of oil and gas wells.

Because real estate and home ownership are key to building wealth, it's no coincidence that minorities' average family income is 60% of the average white family income, with their wealth being just 8% of the wealth of whites. These federal policies that were biased against blacks can be directly attributed to the 21st-century wealth gap. Being prohibited from buying homes in the suburbs in the 20th century and/or outright banned from selling their homes to black people, white people were helped in the 20th century by these racial zoning ordinances. After HOLC came the FHA, which also played a role in keeping certain people out of certain communities; that was the problem. Some still exist today, but let's move on to some solutions that came from this.

The Fair Housing Act of 1968 led to improvements in black homeownership. Slow progress is better than no progress. Fannie Mae has set new lending rules that benefit black Americans. Followed by the Fair Housing Act was the Equal Credit Opportunity Act of 1974, which prohibited discrimination on the basis of race, sex, and marital status, and then the Community Reinvestment Act of 1977, which outlawed redlining after 40 plus years of lost wealth that these communities are struggling to crawl out of sill, and it's 2022. Which did nothing to reverse residential patterns embedded in these communities labeled "hazardous" or "red." Other solutions should include:

- Increase access to down payment assistance like match savings and advanceable tax credits.

- Affordable credit that would extend mortgage and business credit to minority homebuyers.

- Expand government grants that finance affordable home construction.

- Restructure the mortgage interest deduction as a tax credit to make it more accessible to low-income homeowners of color and limit it to low and moderate-income households.

Redlined neighborhoods continue to suffer, and most of us in prison come from these areas. For instance, Baltimore, Maryland, where I'm from, continues to suffer from these redlining policies, with lower rates of home ownership, worse health outcomes, and higher rates of poverty. Baltimore is unique because it is believed that "Baltimore's Ordinance 610" in 1911 was the precursor to redlining across the country in the 1930's. This ordinance was a citywide segregation law similar to the one passed in the 1930's. It is understanding how real estate has affected these communities while also showing you potential investment opportunities, along with potential government solutions that you can back and get behind. What's the sense of complaining about "redlining," "poverty," or lack of real estate opportunity if we don't have solutions to take action on? Knowledge gives you the power to take action. Real estate is the great wealth equalizer.

1031 EXCHANGES

Now, this is one of the best parts of real estate investing. Simply put, a 1031 exchange rolls the gains from selling an old property to a new one. Simply put, it allows a taxpayer to invest the proceeds from the sale of appreciated commercial real estate into a "like-kind" property without recognizing a taxable gain. Investment properties or use in a business qualify as "Commercial Real Estate" under the definition of a Section 1031 Exchange. For example, if somebody approached me to buy a house I own for $50,000 – more than $40,000 more than what I paid. I decided to place the transaction in a 1031 tax-deferred exchange, meaning I didn't have to pay the capital gains tax on the sale. My $40,000 capital gain from this sale was tax-free, as long as the rules for the 1031 Exchange were followed. 1031 Exchange rules require you to invest in more real estate. So, the next logical thing is to use the $40,000 as a down payment on 2-3 more properties. The gain on the sold property is transferred to the new property. One of the most dynamic parts of 1031 Exchanges is you can keep exchanging up to sell and buy double the properties, which means that if you hold them until you die for your kids, all gains are forgiven forever. No taxes are ever due—creating generational wealth for your family and kids. But you can also sell before then and pay taxes at your chosen.

Pro se Tip: (!)

Velocity of Money: How fast can you keep your money moving, acquiring assets, pulling money out of those assets to purchase more assets.

You could utilize multiple types of exchanges, but the most commonly used are for real estate. This includes dirt, buildings, trees, rocks, and water—such as oil and gas and precious metals like gold and silver. Let's back up quickly before I get too deep in the woods. 1031 represents IRS code Section 1031, which covers selling real estate and business personal property. 1031 does not include the sale of securities and shares in corporations, partnerships, and limited liability companies.

To get started on this road, remember that property has to be held as an investment or used in a trade or business to qualify for Section 1031. "Held for Investment" is key when dealing with 1031 exchanges. Simply put, this means you intend to hold the property for future appreciation. To qualify any property for this type of investment, you must hold the investment property for one year and a day.

Types of Investment Property

These items also qualify as investment real estate:

- Timber Rights: The right to remove standing timber from real property.

- Water Rights: The right to remove a certain amount of water per year from a body of water [like a stream or lake]

- Unharvested Crops: Under a different IRS Code Section, unharvested crops sold with land are considered real estate and can, therefore, be exchanged into or out of other investment real estate.

- Cooperative Apartments: If the cooperative shares are considered real estate under state law, you can use an exchange for an investment co-op for any other type of investment property.

- Oil, Gas, and Mineral Interests: This consists of production payments and royalty and working interests.

- Gravel or Quarry Rights: The right to extract rock from the ground and crush that rock into gravel in the case of gravel rights. These rights are exchangeable into or out of other property.

- Leasehold Interests: Qualifies for a 1031 Exchange if the lease has at least 30 years left to run, including extensions.

- Vacation Homes: The IRS states that you can do a 1031 exchange as long as you show investment intent. However, there is much dispute about "vacation homes" with no rental income.

-

45-Day Identification Requirement

From the day you close on the old property, you have 45 days to develop a list of potential properties you want to buy. The "45-Day List" contains the potential properties you want to buy. Whatever property you purchase has to be on this list. The 45-day period starts on the day you close on the old property. The IRS code states, "45 days after the closing date to identify your potential replacement properties."

Your list must be clear enough that an IRS agent can take your list and go directly to that property on the list. There is no need to mess this up because it will throw off your entire exchange. You must submit your list to a Qualified Intermediary handling your exchange. These intermediaries don't submit the list to the IRS. Instead, they hold it pending a potential audit by the IRS.

Also, there is the 180-day purchase deadline, which requires that upon the close sale of your old property, you have 180 days to close on the purchase of your new property, and whatever you buy has to be on your 45-day list. It is important to remember, like the 45-day requirement, that the 180 days start at the closing of the sale of the old property; these two timeframes run concurrently, so yes, once the 45 days are up, you have exactly 135 days left to purchase your new property.

Qualified Intermediary Requirement

One of the most important requirements of the 1031 exchanges is Qualified Intermediaries. By law, you cannot touch the money between selling your old property and purchasing your new property. You are required to use the services of an independent third party called a "Qualified Intermediary." They prepare the exchange documents that the IRS requires when you buy your new property. Next, they hold the proceeds from the sale of the old property until the purchase of the new property [which is important]. They also will act as advisors for the exchange requirements during the exchanges. Lastly, they act as compliance agents that monitor the exchange's requirements.

Pro se Tip: (!)

Don't ever sign a "hold harmless" clause. These clauses say you can't sue your intermediaries if they mess up your exchange. You have been warned!

Intermediaries hold your money in two ways to purchase real estate in exchange. One is a "Commingled Account," meaning they put all your money into one account. It's not a good choice for a number of reasons. Some Intermediaries go bankrupt, and to be honest, they trade with the exchange funds and end up losing most of the money in the commingled account. Other accounts are segregated accounts. They keep all the client's money separate from the funds of other clients. They protect your money from being messed with by the Intermediary. This account gives you its own FDIC insurance fund. For the stated reasons, the segregated account is the best option for you out of the two, so don't settle for less. Of the 2,000 plus Intermediaries in the U.S.A., only 39 are bonded, and only one insurance company bonds intermediaries. Sitting in prison, you have some idea that you want to go home and do this job better than what you read about Intermediaries; the short answer is that you can. Yes, you can be a convicted felon who holds large amounts of money for clients and qualifies as an Intermediary. Look into it and see what changes or different concepts you could bring to this unregulated industry that would allow you to make money while you also help people build wealth through 1031 exchanges.

Compensation for intermediaries comes in two ways. First, they might charge a fee to handle the exchange and the documents involved. [prices: $500 - $1000]. Ensure you get the exact cost because they will be $500 upfront, and then you find out it's another $1,000 once everything is complete. So, get the exact cost for all services rendered upfront. [confirm in writing or email] Others might get paid off interest and an upfront cost. While most Intermediaries are messed up, some of the best 1031 Exchange Intermediaries who provide the best services include:

1. IPX1031.com

2. First American Exchange [firstexchange.com]

3. Exeter 1031 Exchange Services [exeterco.com]

4. Strategic Property Exchange, LLC [spe1031.com]

5. WellsFargo.com

6. 1031x.com

Equal or Up Minimum

The way to avoid paying taxes is to ensure the new property's selling price is equal to or greater than the net selling price of the old property. [Net selling price is the selling price minus the closing costs]. A typical example would be selling a multi-family home for $50,000 and having real estate commissions of about $3,000, title and closing costs of $750, and an outstanding loan balance of $20,000, which will leave cash of $26,250. Now, we need to compute your equal or up minimum. All we have to do is add up two numbers. Debt on the old property that was paid off and the cash from the closing to the Intermediary. Adding these two numbers together gives you the price on your equal-or-up number. In the example above, take the ($20,000) + ($26,250) = $46,250. So, that means that the new property must equal or exceed this $46,250 price tag. When this number is not achieved, you will pay taxes on the leftover gains.

Remember, if you have cash left over after the intermediary acquires the replacement property, they will pay it back at the end of the 180 days. That cash is "boot" [cash or other property added to an exchange to make the value of traded goods equal]. The base amount of the exchange remains tax-deferred, but the "boot" is considered a taxable gain. Loans or any other debt on the property you relinquish and the replacement property must be considered. [ex: If you have a mortgage of $500,000 on the old property, but your mortgage on the new property that you receive in exchange is only $400,000, in that case, you have a $100,000 gain that is also classified as the "boot" and will be taxed.

Furthermore, you must report the 1031 exchange to the IRS by submitting Form 8824 [see index] with tax returns in the year when the exchange occurred. You will need to provide:

- Description of Property Exchanged

- Dates When Transferred

- Value of Like-Kind Properties

- Adjusted Basis [income tax term that refers to an asset's book value change resulting from improvements, new purchases, sales, payouts, etc.]

Lastly, a 1031 exchange should be used for any serious real estate investor as a tax-deferral strategy to build wealth with real estate. There is also another type of exchange called 721 Exchange.

721 EXCHANGE

A 721 exchange allows investors to transfer property held in a like-kind exchange for shares in a Real Estate Investment Trust [REIT] without triggering the need to pay capital gains taxes. Unlike 1031, you can exchange your capital gains into a portfolio versus just one property. The 721 also allows you to get into REITs. But instead of finding like-kind property, you can invest the proceeds with a fund. Ex: $250,000 to invest, instead of finding property under a strict deadline, you could spread that $250,000 into ten funds, giving direct access to and ownership in huge deals while collecting 15% annual returns, such as Private Equity Funds, Title III Jobs Act, Crowdstreet, and ArborCrowd.

721(a) generally provides that no gain or less shall be recognized to a partnership or any of its partners in the case of a contribution of property to the partnership in exchange for an interest in the partnership.

The 721 UPREIT [Umbrella Partnership Real Estate Investment Trust] exchange is an alternative to deferring capital gains taxes without following a strict timeframe like the 1031 exchanges.

721 exchanges have benefits for taxpayers that don't exist anywhere else. Interest for interest on a tax-deferred basis is exceptional. Other benefits include:

- Diversification: Access to a professionally managed, diversified portfolio of institutional-qualify real estate

- Income: Operating participates in the cash flow of the partnership's diversified portfolio of real properties.

- Capital Appreciation: If the real estate properties owned by the diversified portfolio increase in value, operating partners may experience an appreciation of their invested capital.

- Estate Planning: There is potential to reduce or eliminate taxes altogether by transferring Operating Partnership Units (OP Units) to heirs on a stepped-up basis.

[721 Exchange UPREIT]

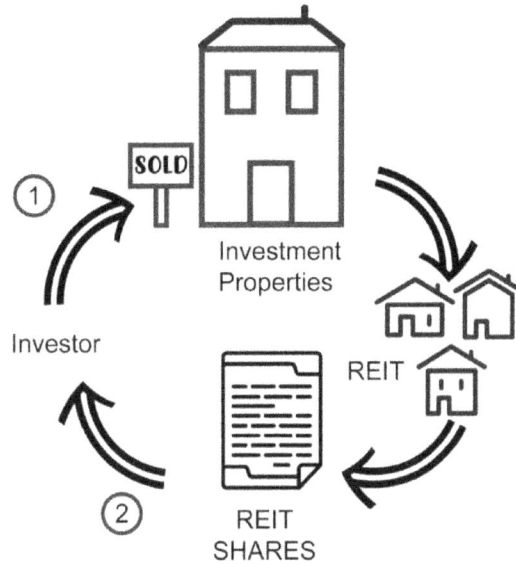

Another special thing about these two exchanges, 1031 and 721, is that you combine a 1031 with a 721 exchange. Combining these two exchanges allows the investor to acquire a fractional interest in institutional-grade property that meets the requirements of the REIT the investor wants to invest in. See the brief composite below:

[1031 + 721 Exchange]

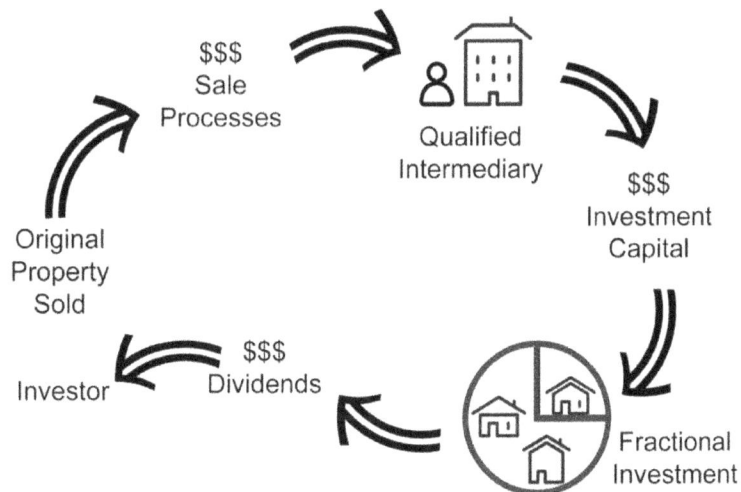

24 Months

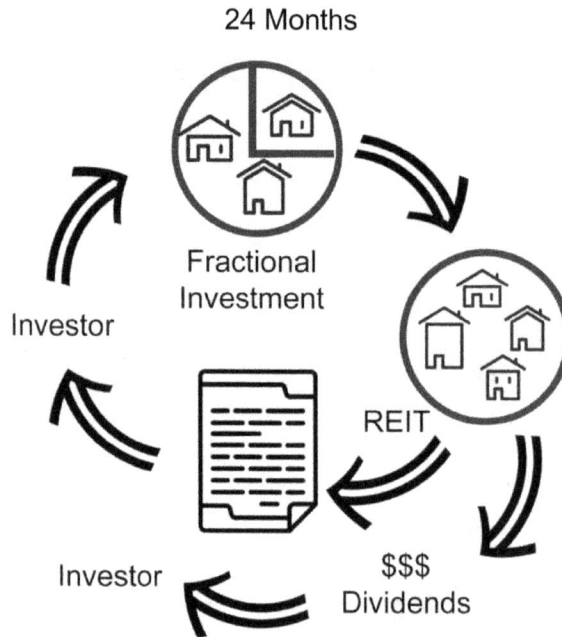

This fractional investment must be held for a significant amount, typically around [24] months, to keep a 1031 exchange intact. The good news is that, as the picture shows, the investment might pay dividends to the investor throughout this period.

After this period, the fractional investment can be contributed to the REIT in exchange for operating partnership units based on the property's value. These units will then be exchanged for direct ownership of shares in the REIT. REIT shares themselves are not allowed to be used in a 1031 exchange. Therefore, once a 721 exchange is completed, this is the end of the line for the deferred capital gains tax. If the share of the REIT is sold, or the REIT sells a portion of the REIT portfolio, the investors will be required to recognize capital gain losses or gains when they file taxes—benefits of combining two exchanges.

We can't expect to build wealth unless we first understand the systems in place to accomplish this task. Real estate offers some of the best options to build wealth, mainly because of tax-free investment vehicles that allow you to succeed. I can write about this so freely because I ate, slept, and breathed financial literacy for two years, and studied the 1% who controlled everything. Information is free, and financial literacy isn't hidden in a safe controlled by the 1%. Learning by reading books is available in every prison in this country because of the 1st Amendment of the U.S. Constitution. But how many of us sit in prison and read about real estate? We all like it and want to own a house, but most never take the time to stop thinking and start reading and applying what you read, then putting into action what you have read. What I write about what I have done and/or am doing. I'm in prison like you, been here since I was 15 years old – over 17 years plus now. Pro se Prisoners don't make excuses, and we take action!

LOANS: MULTIPLE TYPES

Loans are issued by banks, lenders, private institutions, as well as government-backed agencies. The great thing about loans in the context of real estate is the fact that loans are tax-free! Because the IRS taxes income only, loans don't fit into the definition because they're not income. So, let's start with the most common type of loan:

FHA Loans: Mortgages insured by the Federal Housing Administration (FHA) allow first-time home buyers to buy houses with as little as a 3.5% down payment. Even with a minimum credit score of 580, you would be able to purchase a house if you qualify under FHA rules. FHA issues these mortgages and loans–approved lenders in the United States before the FHA homeowners shed out close to 50% of the property's value as a down payment.

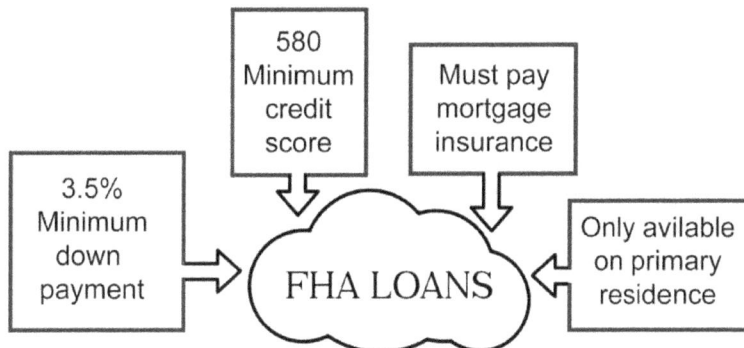

How does this work: You will need a credit score of at least 580, you can borrow up to 96.5% of the value of the house hence, the 3.5% down payment. Credit scores of 500-579 can still obtain a loan, but around 10% down payment is needed. FHA guarantees the loan. Banks do nothing but approve and give it to you. Another requirement is that you must buy mortgage insurance. FHA has five types of loans. They are as follows:

- Home Equity Conversion Mortgage [HECM]: This reverse mortgage program helps seniors ages 62 and older convert the equity in their homes to cash while retaining the title of the home.

- FHA 203K Improvement Loans: repairs and renovations are included in the amount borrowed. Essentially, these mortgages finance both the purchase and repairs of a home. There are 2 types of these 203K mortgages. One is called "standard," meant to help properties needing extensive structural repairs. The cost must be at a minimum of $5,000. The other one is called "limited". It is designed for properties that need only nonstructural repairs. These costs are capped at $35,000. While it's a lot of work for some, what is the benefit of being able to finance the purchase along with the cost of repairs? You can't beat that, but you must speak to your lender before going down this road.

- FHA Energy Efficient Mortgage: This program is like the FHA 203K improvement loan program but focuses on upgrades that can lower utility bills, such as new insulation or solar or wind energy systems.

- Section 245(a) Loan: This program works for borrowers who expect their incomes to increase. Graduated Payment Mortgage (GPM) starts with lower monthly payments that gradually increase as time passes. The Growing Equity Mortgage (GEM) has scheduled increases in monthly principal payments.

- Traditional Mortgage: A mortgage that finances a primary residence using regular FHA loan procedures.

FHA Loan Requirements

- Valid Social Security Number
- US Citizen
- Legal Age
- Credit Score
- Down Payment
- History of Honoring Debts
- Proof of Steady Income
- Sufficient Income
- Tax Returns

Another thing FHA requires you to do is pay two types of Mortgage Insurance Premiums [MIPs] an upfront [MIP], which is paid monthly. Upfront was equal to 1.75% of the base loan amount in 2022. Upfront [MIP] can also be paid at the time of closing, or you can roll it into a loan. [ex. If you get a home loan for $175,000, you'll pay an upfront [MIP] of 1.75% x $175,000 = $3,025. These payments are placed in escrow with the Treasury Department because they are the ones that manage them. Homes that qualify: Principal residence must be owner-occupied for a year.

- Semi-detached houses
- Townhomes
- Condominiums
- I also need a home appraisal from an FHA-approved appraiser.

How To Apply

All you have to do is apply directly with the bank or lenders you choose. Almost all banks and mortgage lenders are approved for FHA loans. But make sure you apply to be "pre-approved" first to see if you qualify upfront before all the other stuff starts dragging you and your family down. Just take this last piece of advice: the pathway for homeownership for people whom the banks would probably not lend to and reject for several reasons. The FHA steps in to guarantee that mortgage loan, and that allows the bank to realize that they will get their money because the government backs it.

Best Investment Property Loans

Because these real estate investments will make their investors a lot of money, it is important to find the right terms, such as a down payment, length of payback terms, and interest rate. Here are some other ways to find financing for your deals.

- Quicken Loans [www.quickenloans.com]: Best in the business for investment lending because they provide nationwide access. Conventional loans from them usually come with a 3% down payment if you qualify.

- Citibank [www.citi.com]: It has a wide variety of loan options and customizable mortgage rates on the website above. The bonus is the low down payment Home Run Program.

- Lendio [www.lendio.com]: All commercial property loans are best. Their marketplace platform makes it easiest for an investor to fill out only one application.

- Nationwide Home Loans Group [www.nationwidehomeloansgroup.com] is best known for its construction loans, which combine up to three loans into one closing process. They also offer the lowest down payment requirements for a ground-up construction loan. Bonus: No payments are due during construction!

- LendingOne [lendingone.com]: Best for rehab loans and makes it easy to get a pre-approval letter. They finance up to 90% of loans to cost while still providing low rates. Loan minimum: $75,000.

Remember, these investment property loans are for you to borrow to buy or build a property that will generate income by leasing and renting space. All the above companies have pros and cons but are the best in their field.

Commercial Real Estate Loan

The first thing to remember is that these loans differ from home loans. Commercial Real Estate is considered income-producing property used for business. These loans include:

- Made out to business entities [Corporations, developers, limited partnerships, funds, and TNSTS]

- Loans typically range from 5 to 20 years, with an amortization period usually longer than the loan's term.

- Loan-to-value ratios are usually in the range of 65% to 80%.

Typical lenders will set out these loans for five years with an amortization period of 20-30 years. So, this means you would make payments for five years on the loan amount, based on it being paid off in 20-30 years. Then, there will be one final "balloon payment" of the entire remaining balance of the loan.

Pro se Tip: (!)

The higher the loan repayment schedule, the higher the interest rate.

Usually, what happens with commercial real estate is that a business entity purchases property and leases out space, thus making it an income-producing property. These lenders look for a few things before lending, such as:

- Creditworthiness
- 3 to 5 Years of Financial Statements
- Income Tax Returns
- Loan to Value Ratios
- Debt-service Coverage Ratios

Use the above teachings to determine what's best for you and your business.

SBA Lenders/Loans

Some of the best loans you could have were loans backed by the SBA [Small Business Administration]. They also have better rates, lower fees, longer terms, etc. Secured by the SBA, provided to you by credit unions and banks. Some of these lenders include:

- Live Oak Bank [www.liveoakbank.com]: Live Oak Bank is the biggest SBA 7(a) lender in the country. All 50 states; broad business loan types. They also top the list with 504 loans. Some financial offers include buying a business or franchise and building or expanding a space, thus scaling your business. Even has high-yield business savings and CD accounts.
- Funding Circle [www.partner.fundingcircle.com]: This is an easy application process that requires only one application to be completed. The maximum loan amount is $500,000, or businesses need to borrow $25,000 or less.
- United Midwest Savings Bank [www.umwsb.com]: This bank makes quick loan decisions and can fund loans in as little as ten days. Its focus is primarily on the medical, dental, optometry, and hospitality business sectors.
- Bank of the West [bankofthewest.com]: It offers an SBA 7(a) loan program for up to $5

million and an SBA 504 loan program for up to $15 million.

- Byline Bank [bylinebank.com]: The country's 5th most active SBA lender. The loan amounts up to $10 million. Offers three business loans. 30 lenders in 10 states. It also has credit lines through the SBA CAPLines program.

SBA Loans

To my understanding, there are four types of SBA loans currently available through several different lenders but guaranteed by the SBA; they are:

- SBA 7(a) Loans
- SBA 504 Loans
- SBA Microloans
- SBA Express Loans

SBA 7(a) Loan

Issued by private lenders but 100% backed by the SBA. 7(a) is a small-business loan issued by a private lender. Don't think you are automatically required to get this type of loan. 7(a) loans are hard to qualify for but have favorable terms and long-term payment terms with low-interest rates. Usually, businesses use them for working capital, expansion of the business, or, most commonly, to purchase equipment and supplies. 7(a) loans have several different loan types that depend on funding needs.

SBA Loan Type	Maximum Loan Amount	Maximum SBA Guarantee	Application Turnaround Time from SBA	Purpose
7(a) Loan		Up to $1,500,000 and 75% for loans greater than $150,000	Regular Business Days	Working capital, equipment and supplies, real estate
7(a) Small Loan	$350,000	85% for loans up to $150,000 and 75% for loans greater than $150,000	5 to 10 Business Days	Funding smaller financing needs.
Express Loan	$500,000	50%	Within 36 hours	Expedited funding for smaller loans.
Export Express Loan	$500,000	90% for $350,000 or less and 75% for loans more than $350,000	24 hours	Expedited funding to enhance a business export development
Export Working Capital Loan	$5 million	90%	5 to 10 Business Days	Funding working capital to support export sales

International Trade Loan	$5 million	90%	5 to 10 Business Days	Long-term funding to expand export sales or modernize
CAPLines of Credit	$5 million	85% for lines up to $150,000 and 75% for lines greater than $150,000	5 to 10 Business Days	Finance short-term and seasonal working capital needs

Maximum term lengths for SBA 7(a) loans depend on using loan proceeds. 25 years for real estate, 10 years for equipment, 10 years for working capital or inventory loans. However, CAPLines of credit can have a maximum term length of 10 years, while it's 5 years for builders' lines of credit, so whatever you prefer, there are options and exceptions to many of these SBA loans. Check with your chosen lender to ensure you get the best loan possible, but it's your responsibility as a business owner to know these things before applying.

To apply for a 7(a) Loan, you must find a lender or bank that's an SBA Lending Partner. National Partners like Wells Fargo, Chase, and Bank of America work with the SBA to supply 7(a) Loans. Start with the bank your business is already doing business with and check and see if they offer 7(a) Loans.

Next, gather all documents and apply to your bank or lender. Application requirements vary based on your lender and what type of SBA 7(a) loan you want to obtain. Some of the documents you will need are:

- SBA Form 1919 [Borrower Information Form]
- Business financial statements, balance sheets, profit and loss statements, and projected financial statement
- Business Certificate or License
- Loan application history
- Income Tax Returns
- Resumes for each business owner
- Business overview and history
- Business lease [If any exist]

After all this is submitted, you wait for approval to close your loan. Some SBA Preferred Lenders can approve your loan without the SBA reviewing it, thus speeding up the review process. The approval time frame is typically 60-90 days. One more thing to look into: If you are a woman, minorities, etc., check out the "Community Advantage Loans" on the SBA website and ask your lender.

SBA 504 Loan

Under the Certified Development Companies/504 program, the Small Business Administration offers loans up to $5 million for business assets that promote job creation and growth. Their focus is on community-based economic development. In order for your business to qualify for this 504 loan, you must operate a for-profit business, have an actual net worth of less than $15 million, have federal income taxes for up to 2 years preceding your application, and have an average net income of less than $5 million; must have a business plan and fall within SBA size guidelines while also being able to repay the loan. 504 loans are perfect for real estate investments and other fixed assets.

Pro se Tip: (!)

Lendistry is a black owned firm that offers SBA Loans, that allows you as a business

owner to obtain capital more efficiently and quickly.

They are used for improvements or modernization of land, streets, utilities, parking lots, and landscaping. It can't be used for working capital or inventory, consolidating, repaying, or refinancing debt. To apply, find a CDC in your area, such as in Baltimore, it's:

Baltimore District
100 South Charles St., Suite 1201
Phone: 410-962-6192

This will guarantee you are dealing with a qualified lender. Also, check sba.gov and put in your business zip code to look for one where you are registered to do business. Once that's done, begin preparing and assembling your 504-loan authorization package using the 504 Authorization File Library to identify the documentation you will need to apply for a 504 CDC loan.

SBA Micro Loans

This program provides loans up to $50,000 to help small businesses and certain not-for-profit childcare centers. While there are restrictions on some things, this program allows you to use it to rebuild, reopen, repair, and enhance or improve your small business. Be aware that you can't buy real estate or pay off debt with this type of loan.

One key difference between this SBA program and other SBA programs is that the SBA fully funds it. This program aims to reach low-income communities and businesses that are often overlooked. The average microloan issued was $14,434, with a 6.5% interest rate. These loan amounts and interest rates can vary because of the intermediaries the SBA uses.

Term Length: 7 years

Loan Amount: Up to $50,000

Interest Rates: 6%-9%

Fees: 3% of the loan amount, up to 20% for loans with terms of less than one year, plus closing costs determined by the lender.

Also, be mindful that collateral is sometimes needed to secure the loan. If you have a small business with no credit history, as most do just starting out, this program is still available to you, as well as people who have businesses with lower incomes. Underserved communities have always been pushed to the bottom when trying to get loans. This program welcomes underserved communities, women, and minority-owned businesses. Because loans from the SBA are very important, you will need the following documentation:

- Personal Tax Returns [two years worth]
- Recent Pay Stubs
- A List of Collateral
- Business Plan
- Cash Flow Projections
- Contracts, Quotes, or Purchase Agreement
- All Business Documents

SBA Express Loan

The last type of the four SBA Loan programs is the SBA Express Loan Program. [www.sba.gov]. The key point about this program is that it offers faster funding! As part of the 7(a) SBA Loan Program, you will have faster funding options, including up to $500,000 in possible funding. The SBA Express Loan Program backs 50% of the express loan. To apply for this loan, you must go through an approved SBA lender and use [SBA Form 1919]. Typical SBA 7(a) loans require a 10% down payment for any loan request over $25,000. However, you will get fast responses from SBA, usually within 36 hours. Eligibility and credit decisions are made at the lender level, not the SBA.

Oh yeah, SBA Express Loans have two types:

- SBA Express Loan: for small business
- SBA Export Express Loan: for small export businesses. The SBA backs 90% of the loan

Requirements:

- Small business
- Operate as a for-profit business in the U.S.A.
- Have reasonable owner equity to invest
- Min. annual revenue
- FICO score of at least 650

How To Apply:

1. Show you invested time and money in your business.

2. Prove you exhausted other lending opportunities.

3. Know your business lending C's [Credit, Cash flow, and Collateral]

4. Connect with a partnering SBA lender.

5. Business plan, financial projections, and assets to put up as collateral.

This program was designed to reduce paperwork and speed funding approval. It can be used for working capital, real estate, and even refinancing debt. When you suggest getting an SBA loan, ensure you do your research and take advantage of all the benefits described above to get the most out of these loan programs. Check out [www.sba.gov] for any additional information you may need.

RECENT CHANGES WITH FANNIE MAE & FREDDIE MAC

The Wall Street Journal recently reported that Fannie and Freddie were changing some policies to make buying homes easier and closing the racial homeownership gap.

Changes Include: Down Payment Assistance, Lower Mortgage insurance premiums, and a Credit Reporting System that factors rent payment history.

Also, they plan to introduce technology that would improve access to credit and make home appraisals more equitable. [Good Idea] Mae and Mac's role in the mortgage market is big; they help lenders issue more loans while keeping lending stable and affordable. Mae also plans to remove obstacles to first-time homeownership and access to affordable, quality rental housing. Mac will focus on credit building and financial education. At the same time, removing barriers minorities face when buying or renting a home and keeping homeowners and renters in their homes. Keep this in mind as you look to get certain government loans and mortgages.

USDA HOME LOAN

The USDA Home Loan is a mortgage program available to rural and suburban homebuyers. Home loans are issued by approved lenders and guaranteed by the USDA—favorable options for rural or low-income areas. One of the last $0 down mortgages with 100% financing means low-to, no out-of-pocket cost to you if you are approved.

Because the word "rural" is defined broadly, more small towns, suburbs, and cities meet the requirement to try to obtain these mortgage loans. With the intent to be lenient, eligibility requirements are low because they want to help low to moderate families purchase homes. With competitive rates for $0 down USDA loans, it's better terms than conventional over-the-counter loans. In order to be eligible, household income must meet certain guidelines, and the home to be purchased must be in an eligible rural area. Other eligibility includes:

- Ability to prove creditworthiness, typically with a credit score of at least 640
- Stable and dependable income
- Willingness to repay mortgage [12 months of no late payments or collections]

See www.usda.gov [for more information if needed]

USDA FSA [Farm Service Agency] Loans

USDA also offers and guarantees loans to eligible disadvantaged farmers. [SDA: Socially Disadvantage]

Below is the latest USDA Farm Service Agency's Fact Sheet to help you see if you fit into or how to proceed with farming. Whether it's to purchase livestock poultry, farm equipment, feed, seed, fuel, etc. A fact sheet provided by www.fsa.usda.gov/farmLoans or also on www.farmers.gov

USDA
United States Department of Agriculture

Farm Service Agency

Loans for Socially Disadvantaged Farmers and Ranchers

FACT SHEET
August 2019

Overview

The U.S. Department of Agriculture's Farm Service Agency (FSA) makes and guarantees loans to eligible socially disadvantaged (SDA) farmers to buy and operate family-sized farms and ranches. Each fiscal year, FSA targets a portion of its direct and guaranteed farm ownership (FO) and operating loan (OL) funds to SDA farmers. Non-reserved funds can also be used by SDA individuals.

An SDA farmer or rancher is a group whose members have been subject to racial, ethnic, or gender prejudice because of their identity as members of a group without regard to their individual qualities. These groups consist of American Indians or Alaskan Natives, Asians, Blacks or African-Americans, Native Hawaiians or other Pacific Islanders, Hispanics, and women.

FSA:

- Helps remove barriers that prevent full participation of SDA farmers in FSA's farm loan programs; and
- Provides information and assistance to SDA farmers to help them develop sound farm management practices, analyze problems, and plan the best use of available resources essential for success.

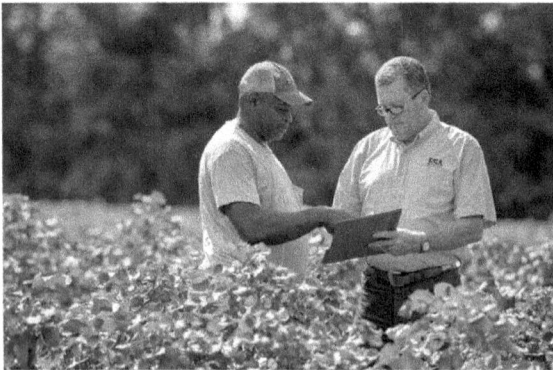

Types Of Loans And Uses Of Loan Funds

Direct FO loans and OLs are made by FSA to eligible farmers. Guaranteed FO loans and OLs are made by lending institutions subject to federal or state supervision (banks, savings and loans, and units of the Farm Credit System) and guaranteed by FSA. Typically, FSA guarantees 90 percent of any loss the lender might incur if the loan fails. FO funds may be used to purchase or enlarge a farm or ranch, purchase easements or rights of way needed in the farm's operation, erect or improve buildings, implement soil and water conservation measures, and pay closing costs. Guaranteed FO funds also may be used to refinance debt.

OL funds may be used to purchase livestock, poultry, farm equipment, feed, seed, fuel, fertilizer, chemicals, insurance, and other operating expenses. The funds also may be used for training costs, closing costs, and to reorganize and refinance debt.

Terms And Interest Rates

Repayment terms for direct OLs depend on the collateral securing the loan and usually run from one to seven years. Repayment terms for direct FO loans vary but never exceed 40 years.

Interest rates for direct loans are set periodically according to the government's cost of borrowing.

Guaranteed loan terms are set by the lender. Interest rates for guaranteed loans are established by the lender.

1

USDA
United States Department of Agriculture

LOANS FOR SDA FARMERS AND RANCHERS - AUGUST 2019

Down Payment Program

FSA has a special loan program to assist SDA and beginning farmers in purchasing a farm. Retiring farmers may use this program to transfer their land to future generations.

To qualify:

- The applicant must make a cash down payment of at least 5 percent of the purchase price;
- The maximum loan amount does not exceed 45 percent of the least of the purchase price of the farm or ranch to be acquired, the appraised value of the farm or ranch to be acquired, or $667,000 (Note: This results in a maximum loan amount of $300,150);
- The term of the loan is 20 years. The interest rate is 4 percent below the direct FO rate, but not lower than 1.5 percent;
- The remaining balance may be obtained from a commercial lender or private party. FSA can provide up to a 95 percent guarantee if financing is obtained from a commercial lender. Participating lenders do not have to pay a guarantee fee;
- Financing from participating lenders must have an amortization period of at least 30 years and cannot have a balloon payment due within the first 20 years of the loan.

Land Contract Guarantees

These provide certain financial guarantees to the seller of a farm through a land contract sale to a beginning or SDA farmer. The seller may request either of the following:

- Prompt Payment Guarantee: A guarantee up to the amount of three amortized annual installments plus the cost of any related real estate taxes and insurance.
- Standard Guarantee: A guarantee of 90 percent of the outstanding principal balance under the land contract.

The purchase price of the farm cannot exceed the lesser of $500,000 or the market value of the property. The buyer must provide a minimum down payment of 5 percent of the purchase price of the farm. The interest rate is fixed at a rate not to exceed the direct FO loan interest rate in effect at the time the guarantee is issued, plus three percentage points. The guarantee period is 10 years for either plan regardless of the term of the land contract. The contract payments must be amortized for a minimum of 20 years. Balloon payments are prohibited during the 10-year term of the guarantee.

Sale Of Inventory Farmland

FSA advertises inventory property within 15 days of acquisition. Eligible SDA and beginning farmers are given first priority to purchase these properties at the appraised market value. If one or more eligible SDA or beginning farmer offers to purchase the same property in the first 135 days, the buyer is chosen randomly.

How To Apply

Applications for direct loan assistance may be submitted to the local FSA office serving the area where the operation is located. Local FSA offices are listed in the telephone directory under U.S. Government, Department of Agriculture, or Farm Service Agency. For guaranteed loans, applicants must apply to a commercial lender who participates in the Guaranteed Loan program. Contact the local FSA office for a list of participating lenders.

More Information

For more information, visit **fsa.usda.gov/farmloans** or **farmers.gov**. Find your local USDA Service Center at **farmers.gov/service-locator**.

While we are on the topic of farming, Bill Gates money manager Michael Larson, has been buying up farmland all over the U.S. for a reason. They can control the Agricultural landscape, which also in turn controls the food supply chain. Let me break down some important facts that will provide an important understanding of why farming is an essential investment.

In the past 30 years, farmland has averaged 11.5% annually in total returns since around 1990. Plus, more humans = less farmland, hence the reason why it's getting so lucrative. Over 30,000,000 acres of US farmland are owned by foreigners [2.5%]. The biggest buyers of farmland are Pension Funds.

Farmland also has low volatility compared to either class of assets. Demand for food will rise from 70% to 100% in the next 20-30 years. Even such things as eggs are up 300% YTD [year to date].

Much of farming is manual labor. Still, you can also invest in it using fractionalized investing, where you can buy pieces of a farm using apps such as [Farm Together App]. It is a good investment because of the high demand for corn and chickens, and prices are increasing. This is just a little general background on the importance of farming in the U.S.

Look at the contents of the Farm Ownership Loans FSA 2001-2016, FSA 2037-2038, and FSA 2302, which show you what is needed for Farm Ownership Loans. See the packet below from the USDA FSA.

CONTENTS OF FARM OWNERSHIP LOANS

- FSA-2001, Request for Direct Loan Assistance

- FSA 2002, Three-Year Financial History

- FSA 2003, Three-Year Production History

- FSA-2004, Authorization to Release Information

- FSA-2005, Creditor List

- FSA-2006, Property Owned and Leased

- FSA-2037, Farm Business Plan Worksheet – Balance Sheet

- FSA-2038, Farm Business Plan Worksheet – Farm Business Plan Worksheet

- FSA-2302, Description of Farm Training and Experience

FSA-2001   Date of Modification: 03-06-2015

REQUEST FOR DIRECT LOAN ASSISTANCE

INSTRUCTIONS FOR PREPARATION

Purpose: This form is used to obtain information from applicants applying for FSA services.	
Handbook Reference: 3-FLP, 4-FLP, 5-FLP and 6-FLP	**Number of Copies:** Original only
Signatures Required: Original by individual applicant(s), Authorized Entity Representative, and/or all entity members as individuals.	
Distribution of Copies: County Office Case File	
Automation-Related Transactions: DLS	

All loan applicants read and <u>retain</u> the top page of the form.

Individual applicants, not operating as a legal entity, complete Parts A, D, E and F.

Individual applicants operating as a legal entity complete Parts C, D, E and F.

Married couples, only one spouse applying, complete Parts A, D, E, and F.

Married couples applying jointly, not as a legal entity, complete Parts B, D, E, and F.

Joint operations with 2 or more persons, not married and not a legal entity, complete Parts C, D, E, and F.

All Entity Applicants and each individual Entity Member complete Parts C, D, E and F. Part C and Part F may be replicated as necessary to include all associated entities and its members.

FSA completes Part G.

FSA-2001   Date of Modification: 03-06-2015

PART A – Individual Applicant, Not a Legal Entity and Married, Applying as Individual

Items 1 – 15 are completed by all individual applicants.

Fld Name / Item No.	Instruction
1A Exact Full Legal Name	Enter the applicant's exact full legal name as shown on a state driver's license or State ID card.
2 Email Address	Enter the applicant's email address.
3 Mailing Address	Enter applicant's complete mailing address. Indicate if the mailing address is different from applicant's physical address.
4A Physical Address	Enter applicant's complete physical address if different from mailing address.
4B County of Residence	Enter the county where the residence is located.
5 Contact Telephone Numbers	Enter the applicant's home, cell, and business telephone number, as applicable. Indicate applicant's best contact telephone number by selecting "Primary" in the applicable box.
6 County of Operation Headquarters	Enter the county where the operation headquarters is located.
7 Date of Birth	Enter applicant's date of birth.
8 Social Security Number	Enter applicant's social security number (9-digit number).
9 Name and Address of Employer	Enter the name, address and telephone number of the applicant's employer, if applicable.
10 Citizenship	Check applicable citizenship status. If non-citizen national, qualified alien, or refugee, as defined by the Personal Responsibility and Work Opportunity Reconciliation Act of 1996 (PRWORA), 8 U S C 1641, applicant must provide copies of appropriate documentation of

Fld Name / Item No.	Instruction
	immigration status, including and not limited, to a current I-551, Naturalization Certificate, or I-688B
11 Race	Check the appropriate box indicating applicant's race More than one box may be checked Providing applicant's race is voluntary, however, if applying as a socially disadvantaged applicant based on race, this information is required
12 Veteran Status	Check the appropriate box indicating applicant's veteran status
13 Marital Status	Check the appropriate block depending on whether the applicant is unmarried, divorced, separated, legally separated or married and applying as an individual applicant
14 Ethnicity	Check the appropriate box indicating applicant's ethnicity Providing applicant's ethnicity is voluntary, however, if applying as a socially disadvantaged applicant based on ethnicity, this information is required
15 Gender	Check the appropriate box indicating applicant's gender Providing applicant's gender is voluntary; however, if applying as a socially disadvantaged applicant based on gender, this information is required
16 For FSA Use Only	Check the appropriate box indicating if information collected was provided or observed
PROCEED TO PART D	

PART B– Married Couples, Applying Jointly, Not a Legal Entity

Items 1 – 11 are completed by one spouse. Items 13 – 23 are completed by the other spouse. Items 25 -29 are shared by both parties.

Fld Name / Item No.	Instruction
1 Exact Full Legal Name	Enter the applicant's exact full legal name as shown on a state driver's license or State ID card
2 Email Address	Enter the applicant's email address
3 Social Security Number	Enter applicant's social security number (9-digit number)

FSA-2001   Date of Modification: 03-06-2015

Fld Name / Item No.	Instruction
4 Date of Birth	Enter applicant's date of birth.
5 Contact Telephone Numbers	Enter the applicant's home, cell, and business telephone number, as applicable. Indicate applicant's best contact telephone number by selecting "Primary" in the applicable box.
6 Citizenship	Check applicable citizenship status. If non-citizen national, qualified alien, or refugee, as defined by the Personal Responsibility and Work Opportunity Reconciliation Act of 1996 (PRWORA), 8 U.S.C. 1641, applicant must provide copies of appropriate documentation of immigration status, including and not limited, to a current I-551, Naturalization Certificate, or I-688B.
7 Race	Check the appropriate box indicating applicant's race. More than one box may be checked. Providing applicant's race is voluntary, however, if applying as a socially disadvantaged applicant based on race, this information is required.
8 Name and Address of Employer	Enter the name, address and telephone number of the applicant's employer, if applicable
9 Veteran Status	Check the appropriate box indicating applicant's veteran status.
10 Ethnicity	Check the appropriate box indicating applicant's ethnicity. Providing applicant's ethnicity is voluntary, however, if applying as a socially disadvantaged applicant based on ethnicity, this information is required
11 Gender	Check the appropriate box indicating applicant's gender. Providing applicant's gender is voluntary, however, if applying as a socially disadvantaged applicant based on gender, this information is required.
12 For FSA Use Only	Check the appropriate box indicating if information collected was provided or observed
13 Exact Full Legal Name	Enter the applicant's exact full legal name as shown on a state driver's license or State ID card.
14 Email Address	Enter the applicant's email address.
15 Social	Enter applicant's social security number (9-digit number)

FSA-2001   Date of Modification: 03-06-2015

Fld Name / Item No.	Instruction
Security Number	
16 Date of Birth	Enter applicant's date of birth.
17 Contact Telephone Numbers	Enter the applicant's home, cell, and business telephone number, as applicable. Indicate applicant's best contact telephone number by selecting "Primary" in the applicable box.
18 Citizenship	Check applicable citizenship status. If non-citizen national, qualified alien, or refugee, as defined by the Personal Responsibility and Work Opportunity Reconciliation Act of 1996 (PRWORA), 8 U.S.C. 1641, applicant must provide copies of appropriate documentation of immigration status, including and not limited, to a current I-551, Naturalization Certificate, or I-688B.
19 Race	Check the appropriate box indicating applicant's race. More than one box may be checked. Providing applicant's race is voluntary, however, if applying as a socially disadvantaged applicant based on race, this information is required.
20 Name and Address of Employer	Enter the name, address and telephone number of the applicant's employer, if applicable.
21 Veteran Status	Check the appropriate box indicating applicant's veteran status.
22 Ethnicity	Check the appropriate box indicating applicant's ethnicity. Providing applicant's ethnicity is voluntary, however, if applying as a socially disadvantaged applicant based on ethnicity, this information is required.
22 Ethnicity	Check the appropriate box indicating applicant's ethnicity. Providing applicant's ethnicity is voluntary; however, if applying as a socially disadvantaged applicant based on ethnicity, this information is required.
23 Gender	Check the appropriate box indicating applicant's gender. Providing applicant's gender is voluntary, however, if applying as a socially disadvantaged applicant based on gender, this information is required
24 For FSA Use Only	Check the appropriate box indicating if information collected was provided or observed.
25 Mailing	Enter applicant's complete mailing address. Indicate if the mailing address is different from applicant's physical address.

FSA-2001   Date of Modification: 03-06-2015

Fld Name / Item No.	Instruction
Address	
26 Physical Address	Enter applicant's complete physical address if different from mailing address.
27 County of Operation Headquarters	Enter the county where the operation headquarters is located
28 County of Residence	Enter the county where the residence is located.
PROCEED TO PART D	

PART C – Entity Applicants

The applicant must be the name of the Operating Entity.

The Operating Entity must complete Items 1 – 13.

All embedded entities within the Operating Entity also must complete Items 1 – 13.

All entity members must provide individual information in Items 14 - 28.

In the case of informal Joint Operations who are operating without a formal written agreement and where no formal tax ID number has been assigned by a taxing authority, the persons requesting loan assistance are to designate which tax identification number will be used as the primary to assign the case number; that number will be entered into Item 4. The remaining Items 1 – 13 will be completed, as applicable. All individual joint operation members will complete items 14-28.

Pages 3 and 4 of the FSA 2001 loan application may be reproduced as necessary.

Fld Name / Item No.	Instruction
1 Full Entity or Trust Name	Enter the entity applicant's exact full legal name as shown on Articles of Incorporation, partnership agreement, as filed with the Secretary of State, etc. In the case of informal joint operations, if the operation is farming under an "assumed" name, please enter the name under which the joint operation farms, otherwise, leave blank
2 Entity	Enter the entity applicant's mailing address.

FSA-2001   Date of Modification: 03-06-2015

Fld Name / Item No.	Instruction
Address	
3 Entity Type	Check the appropriate box indicating the entity type or enter the correct entity type in "Other" if the entity type is not listed.
4 Entity Contact Number	Enter the telephone number which best fits the entity, entity representative, or authorized entity official for contact purposes.
5 State of Registration/ Corporation	Enter the State where the entity is registered or incorporated.
6 Registration ID Number	Enter the entity's registration number.
7 Date of Formation	Enter date entity was formally registered or formed.
8 Tax Identification Number	Enter the entity's tax identification number (9-digit number).
9 County of Operation Headquarters	Enter the county in which the entity maintains its base of operations.
10 Embedded Entity Identifier	If the Operating Entity has 1 or more embedded entities within its composition, check "YES" and completed Items 11 – 13. Otherwise, check "NO" and proceed to completing Items 14-28B.
11 List All Embedded Entities	If the answer to Item 10 is "YES", enter the names of all embedded entities comprised within the Operating Entity applicant.
12 Percentage of Interest	For the Operating Entity applicant, enter the percentage of interest the Operating Entity holds in the farming operation. For embedded entities within the Operating Entity, enter the percentage of interest each embedded entity holds.
13 Number of Entity Members	Enter the number of individual Operating Entity members. For embedded entities within the Operating Entity, enter the number of individual entity members within each embedded entity.

FSA-2001   Date of Modification: 03-06-2015

Fld Name / Item No.	Instruction
14 Exact Full Legal Name of Entity Member	Enter entity member's exact full legal name as shown on a state driver's license or State ID card.
15 Percentage of Interest	Enter individual entity member's ownership interest in the Operating Entity or embedded entity.
16 Email Address	Enter individual entity member's email address.
17 Social Security Number	Enter the individual entity member's tax identification number (9-digit number)
18 Date of Birth	Enter individual entity member's date of birth
19 Contact Telephone Numbers	Enter the individual entity member's home, cell, and business telephone number, as applicable. Indicate best contact telephone number by selecting "Primary" in the applicable box
20 Citizenship	Check applicable citizenship status. If non-citizen national, qualified alien, or refugee, as defined by the Personal Responsibility and Work Opportunity Reconciliation Act of 1996 (PRWORA), 8 U.S.C. 1641, applicant must provide copies of appropriate documentation of immigration status, including and not limited, to a current I-551, Naturalization Certificate, or I-688B
21 Race	Check the appropriate box indicating applicant's race. More than one box may be checked. Providing applicant's race is voluntary, however, if applying as a socially disadvantaged applicant based on race, this information is required
22 Name and Address of Employer	Enter the name, address and telephone number of the applicant's employer, if applicable
23 Veteran Status	Check the appropriate box indicating applicant's veteran status
24 Ethnicity	Check the appropriate box indicating applicant's ethnicity. Providing applicant's ethnicity is voluntary, however, if applying as a socially disadvantaged applicant based on ethnicity, this information is required

Fld Name / Item No.	Instruction
25 Gender	Check the appropriate box indicating applicant's gender. Providing applicant's gender is voluntary; however, if applying as a socially disadvantaged applicant based on gender, this information is required.
26 For FSA Use Only	Check the appropriate box indicating if information collected was provided or observed.
27 Mailing Address	Enter entity member's complete mailing address. Indicate if the mailing address is different from entity member's physical address.
28A Physical Address	Enter individual entity member's complete physical address if different from mailing address.
28B County of Residence	Enter the county where the entity member's residence is located
PROCEED TO PART D	

PART D – General Information

Items 1 – 6 are completed by all applicants.

Fld Name / Item No.	Instruction
1 Counties Being Farmed	Enter the names of the counties which are being farmed by the operation.
2 Acres Owned	Enter the number of acres that the individual/entity owns.
3 Acres Rented	Enter the number of acres that the individual/entity rents.
4A Purpose of Loan	Enter the purpose the loan funds will be used for the first loan requested.
4B Amount Requested	Enter the amount of loan funds for the first loan requested.
5A Purpose of	Enter the purpose the loan funds will be used for the second loan requested.

Fld Name / Item No.	Instruction
Loan	
5B Amount Requested	Enter the amount of loan funds for the second loan requested.
6 Description of Operation	Enter a description of the operation.

PART E – Notifications, Certification and Acknowledgement

Items 1 – 18B are completed by all applicants.

Fld Name / Item No.	Instruction
1 Business Under Other Name	Check "YES" if you or any member of the entity ever conducted business under any other name, otherwise check "NO". If "YES" provide names used in Item 9.
2 Previous FSA or FmHA Loans	Check "YES" if you or any member of the entity ever obtained a direct or guaranteed farm loan from FSA or the Farmers Home Administration; if not check "NO"
3 Debt Forgiveness	If Item 2 is "YES", check "YES" if the government ever forgave any debt through a write-down, write-off, compromise, adjustment, reduction, charge-off, paying a loss on a guarantee, or bankruptcy. If "YES", provide details in Item 9, otherwise check "NO"
4 Delinquent on Federal Debt	Check "YES" if you or any member of the entity is delinquent on any federal debt (i.e. "Federal Debt" includes but is not limited to education loans, delinquent taxes, obligations at Natural Resources Conservation Service, obligations to FCIC, etc.) If "YES," provide details in Item 9, otherwise check "NO"
5 Pending Litigation	Check "YES" if you or any member of the entity or the entity itself is involved in any pending litigation. If "YES," provide details in Item 9, otherwise check "NO".
6 Bankruptcy	Check "YES" if you or any member of the entity has ever been in receivership, been discharged, or filed a petition for reorganization in bankruptcy. If "YES," provide details in Item 9, otherwise check "NO".
7 Employee	Check "YES" if you are an employee, related to an employee, or closely associated with an employee of the Farm Service Agency. If not, check

FSA-2001   Date of Modification: 03-06-2015

Fld Name / Item No.	Instruction
Relationship	"NO." If "YES" provide details in Item 9.
8 Farming Experience	Check "YES" if you are currently farming, or have in the past. If "YES" provide the number of years and a brief explanation of your experience in Item 9.
9 Additional Answers	Provide explanations to any "YES" responses for Items 1 – 8. Use additional sheets as necessary.
10 – 16 Statements	Read statements and certifications in Items 10 – 16.

PART F – Certifications and Signatures

All individual applicants and entity members should read and understand that by signing the FSA 2001 loan application, they become jointly and individually responsible for the information provided within the loan application, and are certifying that the Notifications provided in Part E have been read and understood by all parties signing the FSA 2001.

This page may be reproduced as necessary if additional signatures are required.

Fld Name / Item No.	Instruction
1A-6A Signature of Applicant, Spouse or Entity Member	Enter the signature of each individual applicant, entity member, or authorized entity representative
1B-6B Capacity	Enter a check in the box to indicate in what position the applicant is signing. Entity members will select "self" when signing as individuals. Only the Authorized Entity Representative listed in official corporate or entity documents will check the box marked "Entity Representative." The Authorized Entity Representative also must sign as "Self."
1C-6C Date Signed	Enter the date the applicant signs

FSA-2001   Date of Modification: 03-06-2015

PART G – FSA Use Only

Fld Name / Item No.	Instruction
1 Date Received	Enter the date FSA-2001 Received in Service Center.
2 Date Application Received	Enter the date the application is considered complete
3A Credit Report Fee	Enter the credit report fee and the date it is received in the Service Center
3B Date Credit Report Fee Received	Enter the date applicant paid credit report fee
4 Type of Assistance	Enter a check in the check box to indicate the type of assistance requested. If not listed, specify in the Other space provided
5 Agency Official	Enter the name of the Agency Official receiving the application

FSA-2002   Date of Modification: 08-20-2014

THREE-YEAR FINANCIAL HISTORY

INSTRUCTIONS FOR PREPARATION

Purpose:
This form is used to gather applicants' three years of financial history.

Handbook Reference:	Number of Copies:
3-FLP, 5-FLP	Original and one copy

Signatures Required:
Applicant

Distribution of Copies:
Original to case file and copy to applicant.

Automation-Related Transactions: FBP

Applicants must complete all Items.

Fld Name / Item No.	Instruction
1 Name	Enter the applicant's name.
	Enter the last two digits of the year for which information is provided at the beginning of each column. Complete the appropriate column for the year that information is being provided.
A	**Operating Income**
A1 Crop Sales	Enter the total dollar amount of all crop sales received for each of the three preceding years.
A2 Livestock & Poultry Sales	Enter the total dollar amount of all livestock and poultry sales received for each of three preceding years.
A3 Dairy Livestock Sales	Enter the total dollar amount for all dairy livestock sales received for each of three preceding years.
A4 Milk Sales	Enter the total dollar amount for all milk sales received for each of the preceding three years.
A5 Livestock Product Sales	Enter the total dollar amount of livestock product sales (wool, eggs, etc.) received for each of the preceding three years.
A6 Ag Program Payments	Enter the total dollar amount of Ag program payments received for each of the preceding three years.
A7 Crop Insurance Proceeds	Enter the total dollar amount of crop insurance proceeds received for each of the preceding three years
A8 Custom Hire	Enter the total dollar amount of custom hire income proceeds received for each of the preceding three years

Fld Name / Item No.	Instruction
Income	
A9 Other Income	Enter the total dollar amount of other farm-related income (gas tax refunds, rebates, etc.) received for each of the preceding three years.
A10 Total Operating Income	Enter the total income from Item A1 through Item A9 for each of the three years.
B	**Operating Expenses**
B1 through B24	Enter the expense amount associated with each Item listed in Item B1 through Item B24 for each of the last three preceding years. Include expenses financed with 30-60 day credit, credit cards, and open store accounts. Expenses entered should reflect what is being produced in Part A (Item A1 through Item A10).
B25 Total Operating Expenses	Enter the total expenses for each of the three preceding years separately (Items B1 through B24)
C	**Non Operating**
C1 Owner Withdrawal	Enter the total amount of family living expenses and all non-farm debt payments for each of the three preceding years
C2 Income Taxes	Enter the total State and Federal income taxes paid in each of the three preceding years
C3 Non-Farm Income	Enter the total dollar amount of income received from non-farm sources for each of the preceding three years
C4 Non-Farm Expenses	Enter the total dollar amount of non-farm expenses associated with non-farm businesses for each of the preceding three years.
D	**Financing**
D1 Term Principal Payment	Enter the total dollar amount of principal paid in each of the three years for farm related debts (Do not include payments already included in C1 "Owner Withdrawal.")
D2 Operating Loan Advance	Enter the total dollar amount of the operating loan advance for each of the three preceding years.
D3 Term Loan Advance	Enter the total dollar amount received for the term loan advance for each of the three preceding years
D4 Operating Loan Payment	Enter the total dollar amount paid for operating loans for each of the three preceding years. If you received loans from more than one source combine them to a single total.

Fld Name / Item No.	Instruction
E	Capital
E1 Capital Sales	Enter the total dollar amount received from the sale of depreciable items (equipment, breeding livestock, etc.) and real estate during each of the three preceding years.
E2 Capital Contributions	Enter the total dollar amount of the inflows of capital that are not the result of business operations or other income for each of the three preceding years. Capital contributions usually include gifts, inheritance, lottery winnings, the gift value of substantial asset purchases for less than market value, and the capital contributions of entity members. **Caution**: ensure that capital contributions are not double-counted in capital sales.
E3 Capital Expenditures	Enter the total dollar amount of the purchases of depreciable items (equipment, breeding livestock, etc.) and real estate during each of the preceding three years.
E4 Capital Withdrawals	Enter the total dollar amount of outflows of capital that are not the result of business operations or owner withdrawals for each of the three preceding years. Capital withdrawals usually include gifts, the gift value of substantial sales of asset for less than market value, and withdrawal of capital by entity members. **Caution**: ensure that capital withdrawals are not double-counted in capital expenditures.
F	Signature
F1 Signature	Enter the applicant's signature.
F2 Date	Enter the date the applicant signed the form.

FSA-2003   Date of Modification: (12-31-07)

THREE-YEAR PRODUCTION HISTORY

INSTRUCTIONS FOR PREPARATION

Purpose:
This form is used to gather three years production history from applicants.

Handbook Reference:	Number of Copies:
3-FLP	Original and One

Signatures Required:
Applicant

Distribution of Copies:
Original in case file, copy to applicant

Automation-Related Transactions: (Instructions for writers: provide only the information required, i.e. ADPS TC 3K. If no automation actions are required, insert N/A) FMP

Applicants must complete all items.

Fld Name / Item No.	Instruction
1 Name	Enter the applicant's name.
	Enter the last two digits of the year for which information is provided at the beginning of each column. Complete the appropriate column for the year that information is being provided
A	**Dairy Production**
A1a Herd Number	Enter the average number of milk cows for each of the three preceding years.
A1b Lbs of Milk Sold	Enter the total pounds of milk sold for each of the three preceding years
A1c Average Production Per Cow	Enter the average milk production per cow for each of the preceding three years. The number should be the Herd Number (A1a) divided by the pounds of milk sold (A1b).
A1d Calves Sold	Enter the number of calves sold each year for the preceding three years.
A1e Calves Average Sale Weight	Enter the average weight of calves at the time they were sold for each of the three preceding years.
A1f Number of Cows Culled	Enter the number of cows culled for each of the three preceding years

Fld Name / Item No.	Instruction
B	**Livestock and Poultry Production**
B1 Livestock (Type)	Enter the type of livestock being raised (cattle, hogs, sheep, etc.). For clarification purposes break down the type of livestock further, such as "brood cows," "market animals," "calves," etc., when applicable. Enter each different type of livestock as a separate set of information
B1a Units Raised	Enter the number of livestock that were raised (for the type described only) on the farm for each of the three preceding years.
B1b Units Purchased	Enter the number of livestock (for the type described only) that were purchased for each of the three preceding years.
B1c Total Units	Enter the total number (the total of units raised and units purchased) of livestock of this type for each of the preceding three years.
B1d Units Sold	Enter the total number of livestock of this type that were sold during each of the preceding three years.
B1e Death Loss	Enter the total number of loss due to death for the type of animal described in item B1 for each of the preceding three years.
B1f Purchase Weight	Enter the average weight per unit of livestock that was purchased for sale in each of the three preceding years.
B1g Sales Weight	Enter the average weight per unit of livestock that was sold in each of the three preceding years.
B2 Livestock (Type)	Enter the type of livestock being raised (cattle, hogs, sheep, etc.). For clarification purposes break down the type of livestock further, such as "brood cows," "market animals," "calves," etc., when applicable Enter each different type of livestock as a separate set of information
B2a Units Raised	For the type described only, enter the number of livestock that were raised on the farm for each of the three preceding years.
B2b Units Purchased	For the type described only, enter the number of livestock that were purchased for each of the three preceding years.
B2c Total Units	Enter the total number of livestock (the total of units raised and units purchased) of this type for each of the preceding three years
B2d Units Sold	Enter the total number of livestock of this type that were sold during each of the preceding three years.
B2e Death Loss	Enter the total number of loss due to death for the type of animal described in item B1 for each of the preceding three years.
B2f Purchase Weight	Enter the average weight per unit of livestock that was purchased for sale in each of the three preceding years.
B2g Sales Weight	Enter the average weight per unit of livestock that was sold in each of the three preceding years.

FSA-2003   Date of Modification: (12-31-07)

Fld Name / Item No.	Instruction
B3 Livestock (Type)	Enter the type of livestock being raised (cattle, hogs, sheep, etc.). For clarification purposes break down the type of livestock further, such as "brood cows," "market animals," "calves," etc., when applicable. Enter each different type of livestock as a separate set of information.
B3a Units Raised	For the type described only, enter the number of livestock that were raised on the farm for each of the three preceding years.
B3b Units Purchased	For the type described only, enter the number of livestock that were purchased for each of the three preceding years.
B3c Total Units	Enter the total number of livestock (the total of units raised and units purchased) of this type for each of the preceding three years.
B3d Units Sold	Enter the total number of livestock of this type that were sold during each of the preceding three years.
B3e Death Loss	Enter the total number of loss due to death for the type of animal described in item B1 for each of the preceding three years.
B1f Purchase Weight	Enter the average weight per unit of livestock that was purchased for sale in each of the three preceding years.
B1g Sales Weight	Enter the average weight per unit of livestock that was sold in each of the three preceding years.
C	**Crop Production**
C1 Crop/Unit	Enter a description for each type of crop and how that unit is marketed (bushels, pounds, etc.) for all crops raised in each of the three preceding years. **Note**: Complete a separate section for each type of crop raised, including crops that were only raised for a portion of the reporting period.
C1a Total Yield	Enter the total yield (bushels, pounds, etc.) for each crop described above, for each of the three preceding years.
C1b Acres	Enter the total number acres of the described crop raised in each of the three preceding years.
C1c Average Yield	Enter the average yield per acre of the described crop for each of the three preceding years. Average yield should be the total yield divided by the number of acres.
C2 Crop/Unit	Enter a description for each type of crop and how that unit is marketed (bushels, pounds, etc.) for all crops raised in each of the three preceding years.
C2a Total Yield	Enter the total yield (bushels, pounds, etc.) for each crop described above, for each of the three preceding years.
C2b Acres	Enter the total number acres of the described crop raised in each of the three preceding years.

Fld Name / Item No.	Instruction
C2c Average Yield	Enter the average yield per acre of the described crop for each of the three preceding years. Average yield should be the total yield divided by the number of acres.
C3 Crop/Unit	Enter a description for each type of crop and how that unit is marketed (bushels, pounds, etc.) for all crops raised in each of the three preceding years.
C3a Total Yield	Enter the total yield (bushels, pounds, etc.) for each crop described above, for each of the three preceding years.
C3b Acres	Enter the total number acres of the described crop raised in each of the three preceding years.
C3c Average Yield	Enter the average yield per acre of the described crop for each of the three preceding years. Average yield should be the total yield divided by the number of acres.
C4 Crop/Unit	Enter a description for each type of crop and how that unit is marketed (bushels, pounds, etc.) for all crops raised in each of the three preceding years.
C4a Total Yield	Enter the total yield (bushels, pounds, etc.) for each crop described above, for each of the three preceding years.
C4b Acres	Enter the total number acres of the described crop raised in each of the three preceding years.
C4c Average Yield	Enter the average yield per acre of the described crop for each of the three preceding years. Average yield should be the total yield divided by the number of acres.
C5 Crop/Unit	Enter a description for each type of crop and how that unit is marketed (bushels, pounds, etc.) for all crops raised in each of the three preceding years.
C5a Total Yield	Enter the total yield (bushels, pounds, etc.) for each crop described above, for each of the three preceding years.
C5b Acres	Enter the total number acres of the described crop raised in each of the three preceding years.
C5c Average Yield	Enter the average yield per acre of the described crop for each of the three preceding years. Average yield should be the total yield divided by the number of acres.
C6 Crop/Unit	Enter a description for each type of crop and how that unit is marketed (bushels, pounds, etc.) for all crops raised in each of the three preceding years.
C6a Total Yield	Enter the total yield (bushels, pounds, etc.) for each crop described above, for each of the three preceding years.
C6b Acres	Enter the total number acres of the described crop raised in each of the three preceding years.
C6c Average Yield	Enter the average yield per acre of the described crop for each of the three preceding years. Average yield should be the total yield divided by the number of acres.

FSA-2003

Date of Modification: (12-31-07)

Fld Name / Item No.	Instruction
C7 Crop/Unit	Enter a description for each type of crop and how that unit is marketed (bushels, pounds, etc.) for all crops raised in each of the three preceding years.
C7a Total Yield	Enter the total yield (bushels, pounds, etc.) for each crop described above, for each of the three preceding years.
C7b Acres	Enter the total number acres of the described crop raised in each of the three preceding years.
C7c Average Yield	Enter the average yield per acre of the described crop for each of the three preceding years. Average yield should be the total yield divided by the number of acres.
C8 Crop/Unit	Enter a description for each type of crop and how that unit is marketed (bushels, pounds, etc.) for all crops raised in each of the three preceding years.
C8a Total Yield	Enter the total yield (bushels, pounds, etc.) for each crop described above, for each of the three preceding years.
C8b Acres	Enter the total number acres of the described crop raised in each of the three preceding years.
C8c Average Yield	Enter the average yield per acre of the described crop for each of the three preceding years. Average yield should be the total yield divided by the number of acres.
C9 Crop/Unit	Enter a description for each type of crop and how that unit is marketed (bushels, pounds, etc.) for all crops raised in each of the three preceding years.
C9a Total Yield	Enter the total yield (bushels, pounds, etc.) for each crop described above, for each of the three preceding years.
C9b Acres	Enter the total number acres of the described crop raised in each of the three preceding years.
C9c Average Yield	Enter the average yield per acre of the described crop for each of the three preceding years. Average yield should be the total yield divided by the number of acres.
D	Signature
D1 Signature	Enter the applicant's signature
D2 Date	Enter the date the applicant signed the form.

FSA-2004   Date of Modification 12-31-2007

AUTHORIZATION TO RELEASE INFORMATION

INSTRUCTIONS FOR PREPARATION

Purpose:

This form is completed by the applicant to authorize employers, financial institutions, and creditors to verify and provide employment, income or other financial information in connection with the submission of an application for a loan or servicing assistance.

Handbook Reference:	Number of Copies:
3-FLP	Original

Signatures Required:
Applicant

Distribution of Copies:
Original in case file.

Automation-Related Transactions: N/A

Please read Items (1) through (4) and the Privacy Act Statement. Applicant must complete Items (5A), (5B), and (5C).

Applicants must complete all Items.

Fld Name / Item No.	Instruction
(1) – (4) General	Please read.
(5A) Name	Enter the applicant's name.
(5B) Signature	Enter the applicant's signature
(5C) Date	Enter the date the applicant signed.

FSA-2005   Date of Modification: (03-22-2010)

CREDITOR LIST

INSTRUCTIONS FOR PREPARATION

Purpose: This form is used to gather creditor information from applicants.	
Handbook Reference: 3-FLP, 4-FLP, 5-FLP and 6-FLP	**Number of Copies:** Original
Signatures Required: Applicant	
Distribution of Copies: Original to case file	
Automation-Related Transactions: (Instructions for writers: provide only the information required, i.e. ADPS TC 3K. If no automation actions are required, insert N/A) FBP	

Applicants must complete all Items.

Fld Name / Item No.	Instruction
A	**Instructions to Applicant**
1 Name	Enter the applicant's name.
B	**Creditors (Creditors include any bank, credit card company, individual, supplier, etc. to whom the applicant owes money.)**
1A Name and Address	Enter the creditor's name and address.
1B Telephone Number	Enter the creditor's telephone number (including area code).
1C Account Number	Enter the complete account number for this credit account.
1D Contact Person	Enter the contact person for this creditor (if known).
2A Name and Address	Enter the creditor's name and address
2B Telephone Number	Enter the creditor's telephone number (including area code).
2C Account Number	Enter the complete account number for this credit account
2D Contact Person	Enter the contact person for this creditor (if known)

Fld Name / Item No.	Instruction
3A Name and Address	Enter the creditor's name and address.
3B Telephone Number	Enter the creditor's telephone number (including area code).
3C Account Number	Enter the complete account number for this credit account.
3D Contact Person	Enter the contact person for this creditor (if known).
4A Name and Address	Enter the creditor's name and address.
4B Telephone Number	Enter the creditor's telephone number (including area code).
4C Account Number	Enter the complete account number for this credit account.
4D Contact Person	Enter the contact person for this creditor (if known).
5A Name and Address	Enter the creditor's name and address.
5B Telephone Number	Enter the creditor's telephone number (including area code).
5C Account Number	Enter the complete account number for this credit account.
5D Contact Person	Enter the contact person for this creditor (if known).
6A Name and Address	Enter the creditor's name and address.
6B Telephone Number	Enter the creditor's telephone number (including area code).
6C Account Number	Enter the complete account number for this credit account.

FSA-2005

Date of Modification: (03-22-2010)

Fld Name / Item No.	Instruction
6D Contact Person	Enter the contact person for this creditor (if known)
7A Name and Address	Enter the creditor's name and address
7B Telephone Number	Enter the creditor's telephone number (including area code)
7C Account Number	Enter the complete account number for this credit account
7D Contact Person	Enter the contact person for this creditor (if known)
8A Name and Address	Enter the creditor's name and address
8B Telephone Number	Enter the creditor's telephone number (including area code)
8C Account Number	Enter the complete account number for this credit account
8D Contact Person	Enter the contact person for this creditor (if known)
9A Name and Address	Enter the creditor's name and address
9B Telephone Number	Enter the creditor's telephone number (including area code)
9C Account Number	Enter the complete account number for this credit account
9D Contact Person	Enter the contact person for this creditor (if known)
C	Signature
1 Signature	Enter the applicant's signature
2 Date	Enter the date the applicant signed the form

FSA-2006   Date of Modification 12-31-2007

PROPERTY OWNED AND LEASED
INSTRUCTIONS FOR PREPARATION

Purpose: This form is completed by applicants to indicate any property, including land, equipment and livestock that are owned, or to be owned, leased or to be leased.	
Handbook Reference: 3-FLP, 4-FLP, 5-FLP	**Number of Copies:** Original only
Signatures Required: Applicant	
Distribution of Copies: Applicant's case file	
Automation-Related Transactions: (Instructions for writers: provide only the information required, i.e. ADPS TC 3K. If no automation actions are required, insert N/A): N/A	

Applicant must complete all Items.

Item 1; Part A, Items 1A – 5J; Part B, Items 1 – 7; Part C, Items 1 and 2.

Field Name / Item No.	Instruction
1 Name of Applicant	Enter the applicant's name.
A. Land	Include all land owned, to be owned, or leased.
1A Owner of Record	Enter the name of the landlord or owner of the property.
1B Description	Enter the general description for each farm or tract rented or leased.
1C County	Enter the county in which the property is located.
1D Farm Number	Enter the farm number assigned to this property. (Obtain the farm number from the Farm Service Agency, Farm Programs Section).
1E Total Acres	Enter the total acres owned or leased.
1F Crop Acres	Enter the total crop acres owned or leased.

1G Oral/Written Agreement	Enter "Oral" if this is an oral agreement or lease Enter "Written" if this is a written lease.
1H Crop Share	Enter the crop share amount as a percentage. If you do not crop share, enter N/A.
1I Cash Rent	Enter the cash rent payment amount.
1J Expiration	Enter the expiration date of the lease. If you are not leasing any land enter N/A.
2A Owner of Record	Enter the name of the landlord or owner of the property.
2B Description	Enter the general description for each farm or tract rented or leased
2C County	Enter the county in which the property is located.
2D Farm Number	Enter the farm number assigned to this property. (Obtain the farm number from the Farm Service Agency, Farm Programs Section).
2E Total Acres	Enter the total acres owned or leased.
2F Crop Acres	Enter the total crop acres owned or leased.
2G Oral/Written Agreement	Enter "Oral" if this is an oral agreement or lease. Enter "Written" if this is a written lease.
2H Crop Share	Enter the crop share amount as a percentage If you do not crop share, enter N/A.
2I Cash Rent	Enter the cash rent payment amount.
2J Expiration	Enter the expiration date of the lease. If you are not leasing any land enter N/A.
3A Owner of Record	Enter the name of the landlord or owner of the property
3B Description	Enter the general description for each farm or tract rented or leased
3C County	Enter the county in which the property is located
3D Farm Number	Enter the farm number assigned to this property (Obtain the farm number from the Farm Service Agency, Farm Programs Section)
3E Total Acres	Enter the total acres owned or leased.
3F Crop Acres	Enter the total crop acres owned or leased

Date of Modification 12-31-2007

3G Oral/Written Agreement	Enter "Oral" if this is an oral agreement or lease. Enter "Written" if this is a written lease.
3H Crop Share	Enter the crop share amount as a percentage. If you do not crop share, enter N/A.
3I Cash Rent	Enter the cash rent payment amount.
3J Expiration	Enter the expiration date of the lease. If you are not leasing any land enter N/A.
4A Owner of Record	Enter the name of the landlord or owner of the property.
4B Description	Enter the general description for each farm or tract rented or leased.
4C County	Enter the county in which the property is located.
4D Farm Number	Enter the farm number assigned to this property. (Obtain the farm number from the Farm Service Agency, Farm Programs Section)
4E Total Acres	Enter the total acres owned or leased.
4F Crop Acres	Enter the total crop acres owned or leased.
4G Oral/Written Agreement	Enter "Oral" if this is an oral agreement or lease. Enter "Written" if this is a written lease.
4H Crop Share	Enter the crop share amount as a percentage. If you do not crop share, enter N/A.
4I Cash Rent	Enter the cash rent payment amount.
4J Expiration	Enter the expiration date of the lease. If you are not leasing any land enter N/A.
5A Owner of Record	Enter the name of the landlord or owner of the property
5B Description	Enter the general description for each farm or tract rented or leased.
5C County	Enter the county in which the property is located.
5D Farm Number	Enter the farm number assigned to this property. (Obtain the farm number from the Farm Service Agency, Farm Programs Section).
5E Total Acres	Enter the total acres owned or leased.

Date of Modification 12-31-2007

5F Crop Acres	Enter the total crop acres owned or leased.
5G Oral/Written Agreement	Enter "Oral" if this is an oral agreement or lease. Enter "Written" if this is a written lease.
5H Crop Share	Enter the crop share amount as a percentage, if you do not crop share enter N/A
5I Cash Rent	Enter the cash rent payment amount
5J Expiration	Enter the expiration date of the lease. If you are not leasing any land enter N/A.
B. Equipment / Livestock	Include only equipment/livestock to be purchased, currently leased, or to be leased
1 Owner of Record	Enter the name of the owner of the property
2 Description	Enter the description of the equipment or livestock
3 Number of Units	Enter the number of units of equipment or livestock
4 Rent	Enter the amount of rent you pay for the use of the equipment or livestock
5 Share %	Enter the amount (as a percentage) of the share you receive from the use of the equipment or livestock
6 Type of Lease	Enter "Oral" or "Written" if a lease has been established for the use of the equipment or livestock
7 Expiration Date	Enter the date the oral or written lease expires. If there is no oral or written lease, enter N/A
C. Certification	
1 Signature	Enter the applicant's signature If faxing or mailing the form, print the form and manually enter your signature. This form is approved for electronic transmission. If you have established credentials with USDA to submit forms electronically, use the buttons provided on the form for transmitting the form to the USDA service office. Electronic submission may only be completed if you are the only person required to sign this form.
2 Date	Enter the date the applicant signed the form

FSA-2037

Date of Modification 07-08-2008

FARM BUSINESS PLAN WORKSHEET - *Balance Sheet*

INSTRUCTIONS FOR PREPARATION

Purpose: This form is used to gather information on an applicant or borrower's assets and liabilities, to be used to make loan making and servicing decisions. The agency inputs the information provided in the Farm Business Plan.	
Handbook Reference: 3-FLP, 4-FLP, 5-FLP	**Number of Copies:** Original
Signatures Required: Borrower	
Distribution of Copies: Original in Case File	
ADPS/DLS/FBP/GLS Related Transactions: (Instructions for writers: provide only the information required, i.e. ADPS TC 3K. If none of the systems reference is applicable, insert N/A) FBP	

Producers must complete all Items.

Fld Name / Item No.	Instruction
1 Name	Enter the applicant's name.
2 Date of Balance Sheet	Enter the date of the balance sheet.

A - Current Assets (1A – 1U)

1A Cash and Equivalents	Enter cash on hand, checking, savings, and the dollar value of each. For an entity, enter the amount of cash in the farm business account.
1B Marketable Bonds and Securities	Enter other investments and the dollar value of each. **Note:** Enter certificates of deposit, treasury bills, or any other cash accounts maturing in less than 12 months. Enter any other cash such as hedging account equity or marketable bonds and securities. Do not include IRA or other retirement accounts.
1C Accounts Receivable	Enter all accounts and notes with dollar value that are owed to the producer from business sales or services with a due date of 12 months or less.
1D Crop Inventory	Enter the types of crops and commercial feed held in inventory on the farm or in a commercial storage facility. Enter any crops in the Commodity Credit Corporation (CCC) program with a due date of less than one year. An entry will be made later under current liabilities.
1E Measure	Enter the unit produced (i.e., weight, bushels, numbers, etc.).
1F # Units	Enter the number of units held in inventory for each crop.

Fld Name / Item No.	Instruction
1G $/Unit	Enter the price per unit for each crop as of the balance sheet date. Use local market prices or forward contract prices after adjusting for marketing expenses. The loan rate provides a price floor for grain in the CCC loan program. Therefore, use the higher of either the loan rate or current market price.
$ Value Column	Enter the total value of each crop. (Item 1F x Item 1G)
1H Growing Crops	Enter the types of growing crops.
1I # Acres	Enter the number of acres growing for each crop.
1J Cost/Acre	Enter the estimated input cost per acre for each crop growing. Include costs for seed, fertilizer, fuel, etc. If actual production expenses are not known, standard budget expenses can be used.
$ Value Column	Enter the total investment for each crop. (Item 1I x Item 1J)
1K Market Live-stock Poultry	Enter the type(s) of livestock held that will be sold within 12 months.
1L # Head	Enter the number of each type of livestock.
1M Weight	Enter the average weights for each type of livestock.
1N $/Unit	Enter the market price per unit as of the balance sheet date. Use local market prices or forward contract prices after adjusting for marketing expenses.
$ Value Column	Enter the total value of each type of livestock. (Items 1L x 1M x 1N)
1O Livestock Products	Enter the type of livestock product held that will be sold within 12 months.
1P Measure	Enter the unit the product is sold as, such as weight or numbers (number of culls, pounds of wool).
1Q # Units	Enter the number of units held in inventory for each type of livestock product.
1R $/Unit	Enter the price per unit for each product as of the balance sheet date.
$ Value Column	Enter the total value for each type of livestock product. (Item 1Q x Item 1R)
1S Prepaid Expenses and Supplies	Enter the total value of supplies on hand, prepaid expenses and other inventoried assets. The value used for fertilizers, seeds, chemicals, fuel and oil should be the cost value.
1T Other Current Assets	Enter the description and value of any other current assets which have not been accounted.

Fld Name / Item No.	Instruction
1U Total Current Assets	Enter the total of all current farm assets. (Item 1A through Item 1T).

B - Current Liabilities (2A – 2N)

Fld Name / Item No.	Instruction
2A Accounts Payable	Enter the name of the lender, dealer, bank, or individual to whom the accounts are owed.
$ Amount Column	Enter the payment amount due for each account as of the balance sheet date.
2B Income Taxes Payable	Enter a description of taxes owed, such as State, Federal income and Social Security taxes.
$ Amount Column	Enter the payment amount due for all taxes due, including amounts owed for employees, as of the balance sheet date.
2C Real Estate Taxes Payable	Enter a description of taxes that have accrued on real estate and personal property as of the date of the balance sheet. Include any other levied assessments or taxes that have accrued.
$ Amount Column	Enter the payment amount due for all accounts as of the balance sheet date.
2D(1-4) Creditor	Enter the name of each creditor for notes payable due within 12 months.
2E(1-4) Purpose	Enter the purpose for each note in Item 2D (Item 1 through Item 4).
2F(1-4) Interest Rate	Enter the interest rate for each note listed in Item 2D (Item 1 through Item 4).
2G(1-4) Accrued Interest	Enter the accrued interest for each note listed in Item 2D (Item 1 through Item 4) as of the balance sheet date.
2H(1-4) Payment Amount	Enter the monthly or quarterly payment amount due, for each note listed in Item 2D (Item 1 through Item 4).
2I(1-4) Next Payment Date	Enter the next payment due date.
2J(1-4) Principal Balance	Enter the unpaid principal balance for each note listed in Item 2D (Item 1 through Item 4) as of the balance sheet date.
2K(1-3) Accrued Interest and $ Amount Column	Enter the amount of accrued interest for (Item 1) Current Liabilities, (Item 2) Intermediate Liabilities, and (Item 3) Long Term Liabilities as of the balance sheet date.
2L(1-2) Current Portion of Principal and $ Amount Column	Enter the current portion of principal due on (Item 1) Intermediate Liabilities, and (Item 2) Long Term Liabilities.
2M Other Current Liabilities	Enter the creditor's name for any other liability due within the next 12 months.

Fld Name / Item No.	Instruction
$ Amount Column	Enter the dollar amount due as of the balance sheet date.
2N Total Current Liabilities	Enter the total of all $ Amounts and Principal Balances

C - Intermediate Assets (3A – 3I)

Fld Name / Item No.	Instruction
3A Dollar Value Column	Enter the dollar value of Machinery and Equipment (Item 11H) and Farm Vehicles (Item 12H) totaled
3B Breeding Stock	Enter all types of breeding livestock owned
3C Raised/Purch	Enter (R) for raised or (P) for purchased for each animal
3D # Head	Enter the number of each type of breeding livestock
3E $/Head	Enter the current market price per animal for each type of livestock as of the balance sheet date
$ Value Column	Enter the dollar value for each type of breeding livestock (Item 3D x Item 3E)
3F Notes Receivable	Enter notes that will not be received in the current year, but will be received within 10 years
3G Not Readily Marketable Bonds & Securities	Enter other investments and the dollar value of each. **Note**: Enter certificates of deposit, treasury bills, or any other cash accounts maturing in more than 12 months Include any other cash, such as hedging account equity or marketable bonds and securities Do not include IRA or other retirement accounts
3H Other Intermediate Assets	Enter co-op stock, life insurance cash value, etc
3I Total Intermediate Assets	Enter the total of all intermediate farm assets from Item 3A through Item 3H in the $ Value column

D - Long Term Assets

Fld Name / Item No.	Instruction
4A Building & Improvements	List all buildings and improvements owned and $ Value for each
4B Real Estate-Land	Enter all of real estate-land owned Provide brief description
4C Total Acres	Enter total acres for land listed in Item 4B

Fld Name / Item No.	Instruction
4D Crop Acres	Enter total crop acres for land listed in Item 4B.
4E % Owned	Enter percent of ownership you hold for land listed in Item 4B.
4F $/Acre	Enter dollar value per acre for land in Item 4C.
$ Value Column	Enter value of land. (Items 4C x 4E x 4F).
4G Other Long Term Assets	Enter the current market value of any other type of long term farm asset not listed. Include accounts and notes with a maturity of over 10 years.
$ Value Column	Enter the dollar value for other long term assets as of the balance sheet date.
4H Total Long Term Assets	Enter the total of all long term assets from Item 4A through 4G in the $ Value column.
4I Total Farm Assets	Enter the total value of all farm assets entered. (Total of Current Assets (Item 1U), Intermediate Assets (Item 3I) and Long Term Assets (Item 4H))

E - Intermediate Liabilities (5A – 5H)

5A(1-7) Creditor	Enter each creditor's name for intermediate liabilities
5B(1-7) Purpose	Enter the purpose for each debt listed in Item 5A
5C(1-7) Interest Rate	Enter the interest rate for each debt listed in Item 5A.
5D(1-7) Accrued Interest	Enter the accrued interest for each debt listed in Item 5A as of the balance sheet date.
5E(1-7) Payment Amount	Enter the payment amount due for each debt listed in Item 5A.
5F(1-7) Next Payment Date	Enter the next payment due date
5G(1-7) Principal Balance	Enter the unpaid principal balance for each debt listed in Item 5A as of the balance sheet date.
5H Total Intermediate Liabilities	Enter the total of all $Amounts from Item 5G (Item 1 through Item 7)

Fld Name / Item No.	Instruction
F- Long Term Liabilities (6A – 6J)	
6A(1-7) Creditor	Enter each creditor's name for long term liabilities
6B(1-7) Purpose	Enter the purpose for each long term debt listed in Item 6A
6C(1-7) Interest Rate	Enter the interest rate for each long term debt listed in Item 6A
6D(1-7) Accrued Interest	Enter the accrued interest for each long term debt listed in Item 6A as of the balance sheet date
6E(1-7) Payment Amount	Enter the payment amount due for each long term debt listed in Item 6A
6F(1-7) Next Payment Due	Enter the next payment due date
6G(1-7) Principal Balance	Enter the unpaid principal balance for each long term debt listed in Items 6A
6H Total Long Term Liabilities	Enter the total long term liabilities listed in Item 6G as of the balance sheet date
6I Total Farm Liabilities	Enter the total farm liabilities (Item 2N + Item 5H + Item 6H)
6J Total Farm Equity	Enter the total farm equity (Item 4I minus Item 6I)
G - Personal Assets (7A – 7M)	
7A Cash and Equivalents	Enter the value of personal cash and equivalents
7B Stocks and Bonds	Enter the value of personal stocks and bonds
7C Cash Value Life Insurance	Enter the cash value of life insurance policies Do not duplicate amounts included in Item 3H
7D Other Current Assets	Enter the value of any other personal current assets
7E Household Goods	Enter the value of all household goods
7F Car, Recreational Vehicle, etc	Enter the value of all personal, recreational, or non-farm vehicles

Fld Name / Item No.	Instruction
7G Other Inter-mediate Assets	Enter the value of any other personal intermediate assets.
7H Retirement Accounts	Enter the value of retirement accounts.
7I Non-Farm Business	Enter the value of all non-farm businesses.
7J Non-Farm Real Estate	Enter value of non-farm real estate.
7K Other Long Term Assets	Enter the value of any other long term assets.
7L Total Personal Assets	Enter the total dollar value of all personal assets. (Item 7A through Item 7K)
7M Total Assets	Enter the total dollar value of all assets. Total Farm Assets (Item 4I) and Total Personal Assets (Item 7L)
H - Personal Liabilities (8A – 8K)	
8A(1-4) Creditor	Enter each creditor's name for personal debts.
8B(1-4) Purpose	Enter the purpose for each personal debt.
8C(1-4) Interest Rate	Enter the interest rate of each personal debt.
8D(1-4) Accrued Interest	Enter the accrued interest for each personal debt as of the date of the balance sheet.
8E(1-4) Payment Amount	Enter the payment amount due for each personal debt
8F(1-4) Next Payment Date	Enter the next payment due date.
8G(1-4) Principal Balance	Enter the unpaid principal balance for each personal debt as of the date of the balance sheet.
8H Other Liabilities	Enter any other personal liabilities.
8I Total Personal Liabilities	Enter the total dollar amount of all personal liabilities
8J Total Liabilities	Enter the total amount of Total Farm Liabilities (Item 6I) and Total Personal Liabilities (Item 8I)
8K Total Equity	Enter the total equity. (Item 7M minus Item 8J)

FSA-2037   **Date of Modification 07-08-2008**

Fld Name / Item No.	Instruction

I - Warning

Fld Name / Item No.	Instruction
9A Signature	After reading the warning, enter signature
9B Date	Enter the date the form is signed by the applicant
10 Comments	Enter any comments clarifying information on this form.

J - Machinery and Equipment

Fld Name / Item No.	Instruction
11A Quantity	Enter the number of pieces of equipment to be described in Item 11B
11B Description	Enter the description of the type of machinery or equipment
11C Manufacturer	Enter the manufacturer's name of the equipment listed in Item 11B
11D Size/Type	Enter the size and or type of equipment listed in Item 11B
11E Condition	Enter the current condition of the equipment listed in Item 11B **Note:** (E) Excellent, (G) Good, (A) Average, (F) Fair, (P) Poor **Note:** Do not list junk items
11F Year	Enter the year of manufacture
11G Serial Number	Enter the serial number for each item of machinery or equipment **Note:** Notate if serial number is not available
11H $ Value	Enter the current market value as of the date of the balance sheet
11I Total $ Value	Enter the total of all $ values of 11H

K - Farm Vehicles

Fld Name / Item No.	Instruction
12A Quantity	Enter the number of farm vehicles to be described in Item 12B
12B Description	Enter the description of farm vehicles.
12C Manufacturer	Enter the manufacturer's name of the farm vehicle listed in Item 12B
12D Size/Type	Enter the size, type or model of the farm vehicles listed in Item 12B
12E Condition	Enter the current condition of the farm vehicle listed in Item 12B **Note:** (E) Excellent, (G) Good, (A) Average, (F) Fair, (P) Poor **Note:** Do not list junk items
12F Year	Enter the year of manufacture

Fld Name / Item No.	Instruction
12G Serial Number/VIN	Enter the Serial Number or Vehicle Identification Number (VIN) for farm vehicles listed in Item 12B.
12H $ Value	Enter the current market value as of the date of the balance sheet.
12I Total $ Value	Enter the total of all $ values of 12H.
12J Combined Total $ Value	Enter the combined total $ value of (Items 11I and 12I). Transfer the amount to 3A.

FSA-2038   **Date of Modification 08-19-2014**

FARM BUSINESS PLAN WORKSHEET
Projected/Actual Income and Expense

INSTRUCTIONS FOR PREPARATION

Purpose:	
This form is used to gather income and expense information from applicants and borrowers and used to make loan making and servicing decisions. The agency inputs the information provided into the Farm Business Plan.	
Handbook Reference: 3-FLP, 4-FLP, 5-FLP	**Number of Copies:** Original
Signatures Required: Applicant	
Distribution of Copies: Original in case file	
Automation-Related Transactions: (Instructions for writers: provide only the information required, i.e. ADPS TC 3K. If no automation actions are required, insert N/A. FBP	

Producers must complete all Items.

Fld Name / Item No.	Instruction
1 Name	Enter the applicant's name.
2 Production Cycle	Enter the beginning and ending date of the production cycle and check the appropriate box to indicate if information provided is for projected or actual income and expense.

A – Income (Crop Production and Sales)

1A Description	Enter a description for each crop produced or sold.
1B Acres	Enter the number of acres planned or actually produced.
1C Yield	Enter the projected or actual yield per acre for each crop described in Item 1A.
1D % Share	Enter the share percent of ownership for each crop described in Item 1A.
1E # Units	Enter the number of units *(Item 1B x Item 1C)*.
1F Farm Use	Enter the amount that will be used on the farm.
1G # Units	Enter the number of units for each crop to be purchased or purchased for sale
1H $/Unit	Enter the price per unit for each crop to be purchased or purchased for sale
1I Total $	Enter the total amount for each crop to be purchased or purchased for sale *(Item 1G x Item 1H)*.
1J # Units	Enter the number of units to be sold or sold for each crop.

Fld Name / Item No.	Instruction
1K $/Unit	Enter the price per unit for each crop to be sold or sold.
1L Total $	Enter the total amount for each crop to be sold or sold. (Item 1J x Item 1K)

2. Livestock and Poultry Production and Sales

Fld Name / Item No.	Instruction
2A Description	Enter a description for each type of livestock purchased or raised.
2B Purch/Raised	Check (P) Purchased or (R) Raised for each type of livestock.
2C # Units	Enter the number of units for each livestock.
2D Weight	Enter the average weight per unit of livestock to be purchased or purchased for sale.
2E $/Unit	Enter the $/Unit for each type of livestock to be purchased or purchased for sale.
2F Total $	Enter the Total $ for each type of livestock to be purchased or purchased for sale. (Items 2C x 2D x 2E)
2G Death Loss	Enter the loss due to death for each type of livestock.
2H # Units	Enter the number of units of livestock to be sold or sold.
2I Weight	Enter the average weight per unit of livestock to be sold or sold.
2J $/Unit	Enter the $/Unit for each livestock to be sold or sold.
2K Total $	Enter the Total $ amount for each livestock to be sold or sold (Items 2H x 2I x 2J)

3. Dairy Livestock Production and Sales

Fld Name / Item No.	Instruction
3A Description	Enter a description for each type of dairy livestock purchased or raised
3B Purch/Raised	Check (P) Purchased or (R) Raised for each type of dairy livestock.
3C # Head	Enter # Head of dairy livestock for each type described in Item 3A.
3D Weight	Enter the average weight per unit of dairy livestock to be purchased or purchased.
3E $/Unit	Enter the $/Unit for each type dairy livestock to be purchased or purchased.
3F Total $	Enter the Total $ amount for each type of dairy livestock to be purchased or purchased. (Items 3C x 3D x 3E)

Fld Name / Item No.	Instruction
3G Death Loss	Enter the loss due to death for each type of dairy livestock.
3H # Units	Enter the number of units of dairy livestock to be sold or sold.
3I Weight	Enter the average weight per unit of dairy livestock to be sold or sold
3J $/Unit	Enter the $/Unit for each type dairy livestock to be sold or sold
3K Total $	Enter the Total $ amount for each type of dairy livestock to be sold or sold *(Items 3H x 3I x 3J)*

4. Milk Sales

4A Description	Enter type of milk
4B #Head	Enter the number of livestock to be produced or in production
4C Production/ Head/Year	Enter the production per head per year for the operating year
4D Total Production	Enter the total production per year *(Item 4B x Item 4C)*
4E Price	Enter the current market price for the type of milk produced
4F Sales $	Enter the total annual sales *(Item 4D x Item 4E)*

5. Livestock Product Sales

5A Description	Enter the type of livestock producing the commodity *(Sheep, Goats, Poultry etc.)*
5B Production	Enter the type of commodity produced *(Wool, Eggs etc.)*
5C Measure	Enter the unit the commodity is to be sold or sold, such as weight or numbers. *(Pounds of Wool, Dozens of Eggs)*
5D # Units	Enter the # Units to be sold or sold
5E $/Unit	Enter the $/Unit to be sold or sold.
5F Total $	Enter the Total $ for livestock products to be sold or sold *(Item 5D x Item 5E)*
6 Ag Program Payments	Enter all farm program subsidy payments to be received or received during the production cycle. *(Separate by program)*

Fld Name / Item No.	Instruction
7 Crop Insurance Proceeds	Enter all crop insurance payments to be received or received during the production cycle.
8 Custom Hire Income	Enter income from custom work performed during the production cycle.
9 Other Income	Enter any other farm income received during the production cycle. *(Gas tax refunds, Rebates, etc.)*
10 Total Income	Enter the total income from Item 1 through Item 9.

B – Expenses (11 – 33)

Enter the expense amount associated with each item listed in Item 11 through Item 31. Include expenses financed with 30-60 day credit, credit cards, and open store accounts.

Historical records should be used as a guide. Expenses should be realistic. Expenses entered should reflect what is being produced as provided in A above *(Item 1 through Item 5)*.

32 Interest	Enter the interest expense to be paid during the production cycle. *(Include annual operating interest and all term note interest.)*
33 Total Expenses	Enter the total expenses from Item 11 through Item 32.

C - Non-Operating

34 Owner Withdrawal	Enter the total for family living expenses. Include all household operating expenses and all non-farm debt payments.
35 Income Taxes	Enter the State and Federal income tax to be paid or paid during the production cycle.
36 Non-Farm Income	Enter all income from non-farm sources.
37 Non-Farm Expenses	Enter all expenses associated with non-farm businesses.

D - Capital

38 Capital Sales	Enter the dollar amount to be received or received from the sale of depreciable items *(equipment, breeding livestock)* and real estate during the production cycle.

FSA-2038

Fld Name / Item No.	Instruction
39 Capital Contributions	Enter inflows of capital that are not the result of business operations or other income. **Note:** Capital contributions usually include gifts, inheritance, lottery winnings, the gift-value of substantial asset purchases for less than market value, and the capital contributions of entity members. **Caution:** Ensure that capital contributions are not double-counted in capital sales.
40 Capital Expenditures	Enter the purchase of depreciable items *(equipment, breeding livestock)* and real estate during the production cycle.
41 Capital Withdrawals	Enter outflows of capital that are not the result of business operations or owner withdrawals. **Note:** Capital withdrawals usually include gifts, the gift-value of substantial sales of assets for less than market value, and withdrawals of capital by entity members. **Caution:** Ensure that capital withdrawals are not double-counted in capital expenditures.

E - Warning

42A Signature	After reading the warning, enter signature.
42B Date	Enter the date the form is signed by the applicant.

FSA-2302   Date of Modification 03-22-2010

DESCRIPTION OF FARM TRAINING AND EXPERIENCE

INSTRUCTIONS FOR PREPARATION

Purpose: This form is used by new applicants or applicants adding a new enterprise to provide details on their farm training and experience.	
Handbook Reference: 3-FLP	**Number of Copies:** Original
Signatures Required: Applicant	
Distribution of Copies: Servicing Office case file	
Automation-Related Transactions: (Instructions for writers: provide only the information required, i.e. ADPS TC 3K. If no automation actions are required, insert N/A N/A	

Applicants complete Items 1 through 4B.

Fld Name Item No.	Instruction
1 Name	Enter the applicant's name.
2 Training	Enter a brief description of the training you, or any entity member, have received in farm principles such as farm financial and production management, recordkeeping, and marketing
3 Experience	Enter a brief description of your farming experience, include the jobs, duties and responsibilities you have had in farming operations
4A Signature	Enter the applicant's signature.
4B Date	Enter the date the applicant signed the form.

BEST FARM LOAN LENDER

Farm loans are a critical part of building a sustainable farm for the long term. These loans help farmers buy, operate, and expand their farms. Furthermore, these loans provide liquid cash for the start-up phase to help you establish your farm. Just like a lot of loans provided by the USDA and their lending partners, you wouldn't need perfect credit to obtain these loans. The lender list below shows the best farm loan companies.

- **Farm Credit Mid America**
  www.e-farmcredit.com

- **Ag America Lending**
  www.agamerica.com/land-loans/10-year-line-of-credit

- **American Farm Mortgages and Financial Services**
  www.americanfarmmortgage.com

- **Camino Financial**
  www.caminofinacial.com

- **Farm Credit Service of America**
  www.fcsamerica.com

- **Advance Point Capital**
  www.advancepointcap.com

- **Farm Plus Financial**
  www.farmloans.com

HARD MONEY LOANS FOR REAL ESTATE

Pathways to wealth are forged in many ways, but real estate is the equalizer if properly done right. REITs and Real Estate Crowdfunding allow you to invest passively; some investors may prefer to own outright the properties that are being invested in. Another term these loans are called "bridge loans," are short-term lending instruments that you, as a real estate investor, can use to finance these real estate deals. With the goal of renovating and developing a property, these types of loans are a good fit. Hard money lenders work with brokers to structure loans for you. Unlike bank loans determined by your "creditworthiness," these loans differ because they rely on the property's value to determine the loan amount. They determine this by the ARV=After-Repair-Value, which is an estimate of the real estate's worth after repairs and renovation, thus determining the value of the property in relation to the loan amount they will offer.

Benefits include: Applying for a mortgage takes a lot of time and paperwork because of new laws and regulations. While traditional loans from banks, et., can take months to close the loan, with Hard Money Lenders, this can happen fast, like in weeks. Better negotiation on loan terms always negotiate terms! Hard money lenders remove all the red tape from traditional banks.

- **Concreit App**: You can invest as little as $1. Requires only SSN for verifying identity.
- **Landa App**: Invest in real estate with $5; you can buy property shares.
- Pocket Properties: Buy shares, start with single individual homes.
- **Fundrise**: Crowd Funded Real Estate; start with $10.
- Arrived Homes: www.welcome.arrivehomes.com
- **CityVest**: www.cityvest.com
- **Streitwise**: www.streitwise.com
- **Crowdstreet**: www.crowdstreet.com
- **Acre Trader**: www.acretrader.com
- **Groundfloor**: www.groundfloor.us
- **Realty Mogul**: www.realtyogul.com

- **Caltier:** www.caltier.com

- **Fundrise**: www.fundrise.com

- **First National Realty Partners**: www.fnrpusa.com

- **Akru**: www.akru.co

- **Roofstock**: www.roofstock.com

- **PeerStreet**: www.peerstreet.com

- **Origin Investments**: www.orgininvestments.com

- **Doorvest**: www.doorvest.com

- **Fund That Flip**: www.fundthatflip.com

- **Farmfolio**: www.farmfolio.net

Pro se Tip: (!)

"TIME has a price, because it's precious". -Unknown

BUYING FORECLOSED HOMES

Foreclosed homes are usually owned by banks. Investors love these because they are significantly lower than occupied homes for sale. For a variety of reasons, foreclosed homes sit vacant for extended periods of time, and banks don't care about upkeep or the property, such as winterization, leaks that may occur, or bug infestations. Personal sellers care more about cleaning and keeping the house together than banks. All foreclosed renovations, repairs, and remodeling are left to the buyer because these homes are mostly sold "as-is."

Title policy issues may arise because when you purchase a foreclosed property, the seller is the bank and, more often than not, will not cover the owner's policy. This means the buyer could get hit with both expenses, which could add thousands of dollars to the purchase price. Gaining instant equity from purchasing a foreclosed home is what you want. Repairs and renovations add instant value to the property, even before you rent it out, plus help you justify taking the rent up to make up for these costs associated with the repair.

Financing foreclosures and the repairs are key to you obtaining the property. The Homestyle Renovation Mortgage enables you to borrow to buy a house with a traditional mortgage or get a limited cash-out to refinance the mortgage and receive funds to cover the property's repairs, rebuilding renovations, or energy improvements. There are no required restrictions on improvements to the types of repairs allowed or a minimum dollar amount for any of the repairs. However, remember that when using the Home Style Renovation Mortgage for repairs, those repairs and improvements must be permanently affixed to the property while also adding value to the property. Other important factors to remember before applying for this mortgage for your potential foreclosed property are that the house has to be a one to four-unit principal residence [you must live there], a one-unit second home [like a vacation cottage], or a one-unit investment property. [You can be a landlord]. Plus, you can be an individual living in the home, a for-profit investor, or a local government agency buying existing homes for renovation. You must put down a 10% down payment, including the repair cost and purchase price.

Another great program is the FHA 203K, which I spoke about earlier, which is one of the best and most flexible renovation mortgages in the industry. What's important to remember here is the fact that you can use the 203K rehabilitation loan to tear down an existing structure and build a new one using some portion of the existing foundation. But the problem is that you must use the property as a primary, owner-occupied home. Still, it is a good option if you are purchasing a foreclosed home to live in.

So, if you are interested in purchasing real estate foreclosures to build wealth, start your search here at www.foreclosure.com.

Pro se Tip: (!)

TOP MORTGAGE LENDERS

- Quicken Loans www.quickenloans.com
- AmeriSave Mortgage www.apply.amerisave.com
- Veterans United Home Loans www.veteransunited.com
- New America Funding www.newamericafunding.com
- Rocket Mortgage www.rocketmortgage.com
- Amerivalue www.mortgage.americalue.com

STEPS TO BUY HOUSE CHECKLIST

1. Decide if this is for you.
2. Calculate how much you can afford on a house.
3. Save for down payment and closing costs.
4. Decide what type of mortgage is best for you.
5. Get pre-approval for a mortgage.
6. Find a real estate agent.
7. Begin house hunting.
8. Make an offer on the house.
9. Get a house inspection.
10. Get an appraisal.
11. Ask for repairs or credits.
12. Due final walk-through.
13. Close on house.

All the information provided here will help you start your journey in the real estate arena. Start here, and my next section will show you the next steps in this quest for knowledge. Use all examples and real estate papers that are enclosed herein. Check out the Depreciation questions below.

Depreciation

Frequently Asked Questions

[1] Can I deduct the cost of the equipment that I buy to use in my business?

[2] Are there any other capital assets besides equipment that can be depreciated?

[3] Can I depreciate the cost of land?

[4] How do I depreciate a capital asset (like a car) that I use for both business and personal?

[5] If I owe money on an asset, can I still depreciate it?

[6] Can I claim depreciation on equipment that I rent or lease for my business?

[7] I have owned a building for several years and made major improvements to it this year. Can I deduct the cost of those improvements?

[8] What information do I need to compute depreciation on my capital assets?

[9] What is basis?

[10] What is class life?

[11] Why is the term "placed in service" important?

[12] What method of depreciation should I use?

[13] How does the month I place my equipment in service affect my depreciation computation?

[14] Does the month I place my building in service affect my depreciation computation?

[15] Is there any exception to the general rule that costs of property must be depreciated?

[16] Are there any limitations on the amount of depreciation I can claim in one year?

[17] Can I claim depreciation on my business vehicle if I use the standard mileage rate?

[18] How do I claim depreciation on my tax return?

[1] Can I deduct the cost of the equipment that I buy to use in my business?

Equipment is considered a capital asset. You can deduct the cost of a capital asset, but not all at once. The general rule is that you depreciate the asset by deducting a portion of the cost on your tax return over several years. See Question 15 for an exception to this general rule.

Return to top

[2] Are there any other capital assets besides equipment that can be depreciated?

There are several types of capital assets that can be depreciated when you use them in your business. For example:

- *Real Property*- buildings or anything else built on or attached to land
- *Personal Property* – cars, trucks, equipment, furniture, or almost anything that isn't "real property"

Return to top

[3] Can I depreciate the cost of land?

Land can never be depreciated. Since land cannot be depreciated, you need to allocate the original purchase price between land and building. You can use the property tax assessor's values to compute a ratio of the value of the land to the building.

Example:

Ryan bought an office building for $100,000. The property tax statement shows:

Improvements	$60,000	75%
Land	$20,000	25%
Total Value	$80,000	100%

Multiply the purchase price ($100,000) by 25% to get a land value of $25,000. You can depreciate your $75,000 basis in the building using the mid-month MACRS tables.

Return to top

[4] How do I depreciate a capital asset (like a car) that I use for both business and personal?

Only the business portion of the asset can be depreciated on your tax return. For example, if you use your car 60% for business use, depreciation can be claimed on 60% of the cost.

Return to top

[5] If I owe money on an asset, can I still depreciate it?

Yes, as long as you are responsible for making payments on the asset, you can take a depreciation deduction.

Return to top

[6] Can I claim depreciation on equipment that I rent or lease for my business?

If you are renting or leasing an asset, you can deduct your monthly rent/lease costs as an expense. Usually only the owner can depreciate a capital asset.

―

Property is placed in service when it is ready and available for use in your business even if you have not begun using it. This date determines when you can begin to depreciate the asset.

Return to top

[12] What method of depreciation should I use?

The method used by most taxpayers is the Modified Accelerated Cost Recovery System (MACRS). MACRS provides a uniform method for all taxpayers to compute the depreciation. Using the basis, class life, and the MACRS tables, you can compute the deduction for each asset in the year it is placed in service and each subsequent year of its class life. See Publication 946, How to Depreciate Property.

Example:

Shawn bought and placed in service a used pickup for $15,000 on March 5, 1998. The pickup has a 5 year class life. His depreciation deduction for each year is computed in the following table.

Year	Cost x MACRS %	Depreciation
1998	$15,000 x 20.00%	$3,000
1999	$15,000 x 32.00%	$4,800
2000	$15,000 x 19.20%	$2,880
2001	$15,000 x 11.52%	$2,880
2002	$15,000 x 11.52%	$2,880
2003	$15,000 x 5.76%	$ 864
Total		$15,000

MACRS Percentage Table

Year	3 Year	5 Year	7 Year
1	33.33%	20.00%	14.29%
2	44.45%	32.00%	24.49%
3	14.81%	19.20%	17.49%
4	7.41%	11.52%	12.49%
5		11.52%	8.93%
6		5.76%	8.92%
7			8.93%
8			4.46%

Return to top

[13] How does the month I place my equipment in service affect my depreciation computation?

MACRS assumes all *personal property* is purchased and placed in service in the middle of the year. This is called the half-year convention. The example in Question 12 and the MACRS percentage table above show how to compute depreciation using the half-year convention.

There is an exception to the half-year convention. If more than 40% of your newly purchased *personal property* is placed in service during the last 3 months of a year, then you should use the mid-quarter convention. The mid-quarter convention tables start your depreciation in the quarter that you placed the asset in service. The mid-quarter convention reduces the amount of the depreciation for the year because you are only using the property for a short period of time. If you are required to use the mid-quarter convention, those MACRS tables can be found in Publication 946, How to Depreciate Property.

Return to top

[14] Does the month I place my building in service affect my depreciation computation?

Depreciation on *real property*, like an office building, begins in the month the building is placed in service. This is called the mid-month convention. In most cases, when you buy a building, the purchase price includes the cost of both the land and the building. Since land cannot be depreciated, you need to identify the portion of the original purchase price that relates to land. You can use the property tax assessor's values to compute a ratio of the value of the land to the building. The MACRS tables for mid-month convention are in Publication 946, How to Depreciate Property.

Example:

Ryan bought an office building for $100,000. The property tax statement shows :

Improvements	$60,000	75%
Land	$20,000	25%
Total Value	$80,000	100%

Multiply the purchase price ($100,000) by 25% to get a land value of $25,000. You can depreciate your $75,000 basis in the building using the mid-month MACRS tables.

Return to top

[15] Is there any exception to the general rule that costs of property must be depreciated?

This exception is called *Section 179 Deduction*. You can choose to take an immediate deduction for some personal property that you would otherwise depreciate over several years. You must make this election in the year that you placed the property in service using Form 4562, Depreciation and Amortization. You cannot take this special deduction on property you've previously used personally and then converted to business use.

This deduction is limited to your wages and net business income. There is also a maximum dollar limit, which changes from year to year. The maximum dollar limitation is printed on Form 4562 every year. If you can't use all of the *Section 179 Deduction* because of the income limit, you can carry the unused deduction over to the next tax year.

Example:

Mark purchased a piece of equipment for $30,000 in 1998. On his 1998 tax return he could choose to take an *additional* depreciation deduction up to $17,500. Mark's total business net profit for 1998 was $12,000. His *additional* first year deduction would be limited to $12,000. If he elects the full $17,500, the unused $5,500 ($17,500-$12,000) will be carried over to 1999.

Return to top

[16] Are there any limitations on the amount of depreciation I can claim in one year?

There are not any overall limitations on yearly depreciation. However, if an asset is considered *Listed Property*, your annual deduction is limited. Listed property is a term for business assets that are often used for personal purposes. Under the MACRS rules, depreciation is limited for listed property, such as:

- Vehicles that weigh 6,000 or less
- Other property used for transportation (pick-ups, airplanes, buses, boats, motorcycles, etc.)
- Property used for entertainment, recreation, or amusement (video recorders, stereo equipment, photographic equipment, etc.)
- Computer and related equipment unless used at a regular place of business
- Cellular telephones

Return to top

[17] Can I claim depreciation on my business vehicle if I use the standard mileage rate?

The standard mileage rate covers all the expenses of operating your vehicle. Therefore you do not claim depreciation seperately. However, if you use the actual expense method (see the Travel and Entertainment FAQ's) to compute your vehicle expenses, you will be allowed to claim depreciation.

Example:

Dianne uses her Corvette in her business. She took odometer reading at the beginning and end of the year. The total miles for the year were 12,000. She kept a log to record her business miles. The car cost $64,000.

Business Miles	7,000
Total Miles	12,000
Business Percentage (7000/12000)	58%
Original Cost	$64,000
Business Use Percentage	58%
Basis to be Depreciated	$37,334
MACRS percentage	20%
Maximum MACRS Depreciation	$ 7,467
Maximum Vehicle Depreciation (see Publication 946)	$ 3,160
Business Use Percentage	58%
Limited Vehicle Depreciation	$1,843

Dianne compares the maximum MACRS depreciation with the limited vehicle depreciation. She can deduct the smaller of the two which is $1,843.

Return to top

[18] How do I claim depreciation on my tax return?

You must complete and attach Form 4562 to your tax return if you are claiming any of the following:

- A Section 179 deduction for the current year or a Section 179 carryover deduction from a prior year
- Depreciation for property placed in service during the current year
- Depreciaiton on any vehicle or other listed property, regardless of when it was placed in service

Return to top

BUSINESS FORMATION FOR WEALTH BUILDING

Forming a business is one of the first steps in wealth building. Sitting in prison, you must be wondering how you are going to form a business in the world from prison. Other prisoners have probably told you that you can't do it! I love the guy around prison who always be like, "They are not going to let you do that." Instead of asking how you can do something or investing in some educational material so that they come out with you with an educated answer, they suck the energy and time out of the room. Avoid them! I was told that before, so what started out as a time-stealing conversation ended with me showing them how to start an LLC from prison. Prisons have rules about operating a business within prison or obtaining mail from your business through the mail. Some just want to know what you are doing and want you to seek approval. Even those rules are not sold because DOC can't restrict you from owning a company outside of prison that your state authorizes you to obtain. While in prison, I started and own Awood Investment Group, LLC, which invests in multiple sectors, and it holds all my stock, cryptocurrency, and Forex trading positions. This was established while in prison using federal and state laws, which even DOC can't override in their continued advances on our rights. Wealth building must include owning a business or businesses for investment purposes. The only reason the U.S. economy works is because of "employees"! So, the government wants to create as many jobs as possible to allow for tax revenue and other social net programs funded by tax revenue from employee checks. While this is true of most countries around the world, the U.S.A. gives businesses a lot of deductions, which, as you will see, if managed correctly, can be used to offset the income from the business.

FORMING YOUR BUSINESS ENTITY

There are several entities that can be formed to be considered a business. Let's start from the top: SOLE PROPRIETORSHIPS.

- One owner business

- Taxes not legally separate from the owner

- Losses and business income reported on individual tax return

- Must use both (form 1040) and include (Schedule C) for all business Profit/Losses

- Business losses can offset any taxable income you have earned from other sources (up to 2 years)

- Can be liable from other sources (up to 2 years)

- Can be liable personally for all business-related obligations.

- Insurance offers protection against lawsuits or other claims against the business itself.

- Register business by filing a [state] Fictitious Business Name Form [See Example Form – Index]

- Register with City Tax registration.

- Must pay federal and state taxes on income on profits (business), including any funds kept in the business for expansion.

- IRS Form 1040 (Income you earned at job) (Sample in index)

- IRS Schedule C (All Business Profits) (Sample in index)

- IRS Schedule SE (Self Employment tax) (Sample in index)

- Schedule C submitted once a year, with your 1040 form (April 15 deadline)

- If you own several businesses as a Sole Proprietorship, each business must file a separate Schedule C.

- If you make under $400 profit in a business year, you don't have to file, but since this is the government, do so anyway.

- Remember, if you lose money in any year, you can deduct that loss from any other income you make for that year by filing Schedule C. This will allow you to reduce your taxable income.

- IRS Schedule C-EZ (for extra small sole proprietorships)

- As a Sole Proprietorship, you have to estimate your taxes for the year and pay them in quarterly installments.

- Self-employment tax must be paid, with a tax rate of 15.3%, of which 12.4% goes towards social security and 2.5% goes towards Medicare. (Medicare is calculated upon total profits) (Social Security is capped at a certain amount each year).

- ½ of the total self-employment tax can be deducted from taxable income at year-end. Remember, under $400 a year, you don't have to pay the self-employment tax. Report self-employment tax on (Schedule SE), look at the 1040 form "other taxes" section, and add it to your personal tax commitment

For all forms for sole proprietorship, check out the index section at the back of the book.

Forming LLC

- The first step is to file Articles of Organization with the Secretary of State of the state where you wish to start the LLC.

- Maryland—where I'm at—has a web portal also called "Maryland Business Express," where all you have to do is fill out the forms online and pay the $140 fee. You can also set up your outside contact online if you choose, or just write to your Secretary of State to get a copy of the "Articles of Organization."

- Fill out all the necessary info, but remember that you can't use the prison address for a business address (more on addresses later).

- Next, you should also draw up an "Operating Agreement," which governs the internal workings of your LLC.

- There will be a filing fee and sometimes annual dues (depending on the state).

- You must obtain a "Free" EIN from the IRS. Don't ever pay for this number; it's free at irs.gov/ein. This is your Employer Identification Number, which is used to identify a business entity for tax purposes.

- You will also need someone you trust to be the LLC's "Registered Agent." This person will be authorized to accept important legal documents on the business's behalf.

- Oh yeah, there is one more thing about obtaining your EIN. Make sure all information is the same on your LLC and EIN paperwork. EVERYTHING! Applying can be done online – print all confirmation documents or by fax, which will require you to complete (Form SS-4) and fax it to (855)-641-6935; attach a fax number, and you will get it in (4) four business days. By mail is the longest process, taking up to 4 weeks. Again, you will need (Form SS-4) (See sample in index), and it needs to be mailed to:

Internal Revenue Service
Attn: EIN Operation
Cincinnati, OH 45999

- All documents with numbers will be mailed back to the address on file. The simplest way to obtain one is by simply calling by phone (outside contact) for you. Phone 800-829-1040, select a language, and select option three (3) for business taxes. Use your registered agent to place a call because the LLC must authorize that person to apply. Ensure they have a blank copy of Form SS-4 so they can properly answer the questions by the IRS. After that, the IRS agent will give you the EIN over the phone.

- The DUNS number is another important number that needs to be obtained. Before applying for a DUNS number, complete all the steps above because you will need it when getting your DUNS number.

- DUNs are issued by Dun & Bradstreet, the largest nationwide business credit reporting agency. Obtaining this number allows you to start building your business credit and allows your business to borrow money without a personal guarantor. This number is also "FREE". Never get tricked into buying this number. It usually takes up to 30 days to get, but this is the United States; for a fee, you can expedite the process all the way down to 5-7 business days. Visit www.fedgov.dnb.com, and make sure your registered agent for your LLC or the manager of the LLC does this. Once you are on the site, check to see if your business (LLC) is listed already; if so, you can call the number listed on the site to obtain the DUNS number. Select "Get Your Free DUNS" if you're not listed, and follow all the steps to complete the form.

- Profits and losses are reported on Form 1065, and no tax is paid with this return, which is due April 15.

- Must submit Form 1065, Schedule K-1, to the IRS for each member share or profit and losses if more than one member is a part of the LLC

Pro se Tip: (!)

Quarterly Due Dates

Income Made During	Tax Installment Due
Jan 1 thru March 31	April 15th
April 1 thru May 31	June 15th
June 1 thru Aug 31	Sept 15th
Sept 1 thru Dec 31	Jan 15th of the next year

- Expect to owe $1,000 to the IRS at year-end, above and beyond any taxes withheld from wages. This comes out to about $3,000 to $6,000 in adjusted gross income from your business. But if your business is barely breaking even, you probably, more than likely, do not have to make estimated payments according to the chart above. So, just estimate your taxes for the year from your business, and if you expect to owe at least $1,000, as noted before, then you must follow the chart above and pay the quarterly installments.

Forming C-Corp

- A corporation is a legal entity that is separate from its owner.
- Corporations must be created under the state's laws and regulated by state law.
- Shareholders are not liable personally for the company's debt.
- Corporations can also be created by one person or a group of people.
- Those groups of people or persons must be incorporated to be officially created as Corporations under the law.
- Most states will want you to file "Articles of Incorporation" (see sample in index)
- Once you are incorporated, stocks must be issued to shareholders.
- After that, the shareholders must elect a "Board of Directors" in the "Annual Meeting".
- The Board oversees and hires the Senior Management while executing the Business Plan, so choose these Board Members wisely.
- Stock from the corporation is basically equity (i.e., security) that represents the ownership of a part of the issuing corporation (i.e., the one you form).

Structure Diagram

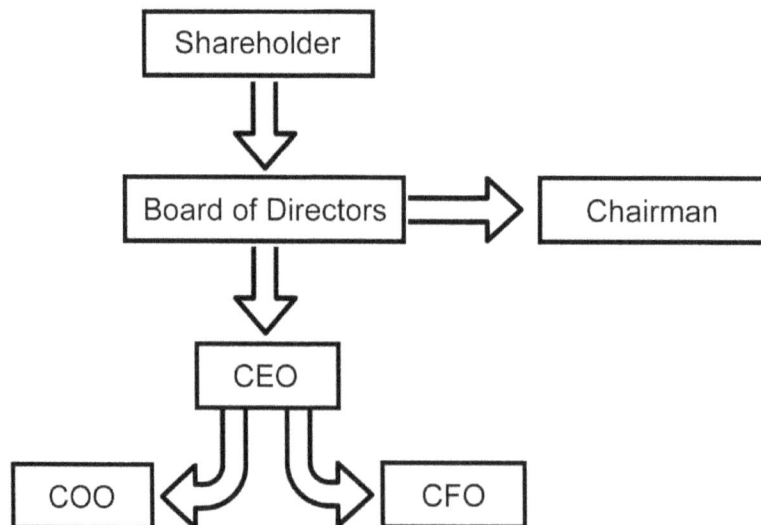

- If you don't want to set up these entities on your own through your state Secretary of State, there are other options, such as easy-to-use websites that will do everything, even some that will set up bank accounts, website domains, etc. Simply pay their fee ($) and the state fee ($), and they will set it up for you. Below is the list; they also set up LLCs, Sole Proprietorships, etc.

Websites for Entity Set-Up

- ○ www.legalzoom
- ○ www.incfile.com √
- ○ www.swiftfilings.com
- ○ www.zenbusiness.com
- ○ www.tailorbrands.com

- Get your outside contact to look up the best ones based on their offering www.incfile.com is my favorite because they set up everything, including the business bank account for your LLC or C-Corp. These are the important breakdowns of the structures of businesses; now, let's go through how being an owner of a business helps you build vast amounts of wealth. Management of your business is key to how far you go, so understanding the financial management process is key to proper wealth building.

FINANCIAL MANAGEMENT PROCESS

We will start with a list that will show you step-by-step the process of managing your financials. This is important not only for the health of your business and to see where future growth is but also to remember that we are building wealth, so knowing the financials is important to document for tax purposes.

1. Keep Records

2. Enter Information in the Bookkeeping System (QuickBooks, etc.)

3. Generate Financial Reports (Profit/Loss)

4. Open a Business Bank Account

5. Keeping and Organizing (Receipts)

6. Income Receipts & Expenditure Receipts

7. Financial Reports (create)
    Profit & Loss Formula:
    Sales Revenue
    (–) Variable Costs (cost of sale)
    (–) Gross Profit (gross margins)
    (–) Fixed Costs
    (–) Net Profit (See index for sample)

8. Cash Flow Formula
    8 Cash in the bank out at the beginning of the month
    (x) Cash receipts for the month
    (–) Cash disbursements for the month
    (=) Cash in the bank at the end of the month
    (Sample cash flow chart in index)

9. Balance Sheet
    A balance Sheet is a financial report showing the net worth of your business at a particular point in time. (sample balance sheet in index)

(Assets – Liabilities = Equity)

Things Business Owes

Anything of Monetary Value

What's left over when your subtract liabilities from assets.

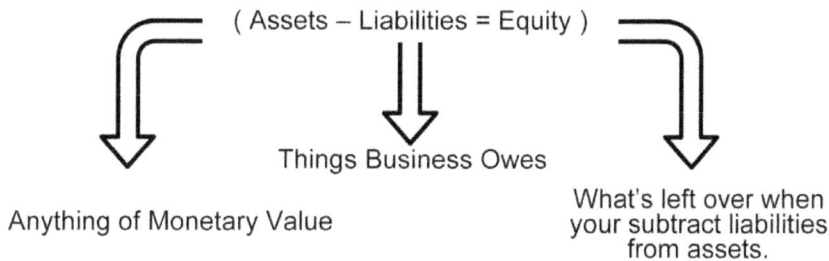

10. Technology to manage money and inventory.

- Spreadsheets

- Point of Sales (POS) Systems

- Project Management (CRM) Software

- Database Programs: FileMaker Pro or Microsoft Access

Also, at the end of the book is a glossary defining Accounting, Real Estate, etc. Knowing the difference between an "Account Payable" and an "Account Receivable" is important to you and your future business. The knowledge you need financially to go out in the world and succeed is all in here for you. What the wealthy know and use, now you know and can use. Wealth is created through knowledge first. There are too many possibilities out there to be doing the same thing that caused you to come to prison in the first place. Getting good grades in school or having a high-paying job doesn't make you wealthy. Understanding money is the key to wealth, even if it starts with reading and gaining the knowledge of proper financial management.

Pro se Tip: (!)

POWER: The ability to shape and influence life's circumstances.

BUSINESS PLAN

Below, you will find a sample copy of a business plan that you can use as a reference to develop your own plan for your business. A business plan defines in detail a company's objectives and how it will achieve them. It shows your company's core business activities and is commonly used by start-up companies to get off the ground. Follow all the steps below and develop your plans for your company/business. More importantly, you will need this to get loans from banks and other lenders.

Your Company Name

Business Plan

Address Line 1
Address Line 2
City, ST ZIP Code
Telephone
Fax
E-Mail

Table of Contents

I.   Executive Summary

This should be a summary of all other sections.

We suggest this section be prepared last.

1. Describe the business you are in, what product or service you sell, and the market you will be serving.

2. Describe the legal structure of the business: sole proprietor, partnership, LLC, or corporation.

(Proof of paperwork should be attached as supporting documents)

3. Describe the history of your business - How you developed the idea to start a new business.

4. Describe your experience in the business/industry and how it will help you succeed.

5. Describe your reason for believing the business will succeed.

6. Address Funding- 1st year anticipated sales, how much money you have already put into the business (if any), discuss any need for funding, and what will funding be used for.

II.   Marketing Plan

1. Describe your products and services.
   * If you are selling retail products, list and include a brief description of each one.
   * What are the features and benefits of your products or services?
   * How will your product be made or how will your services be provided?
   * Who will supply the materials?
   * What future products/services will you offer, when?
   * What specific need or want is being fulfilled by   your product(s)/service(s)?

2. Distribution
   * How will your products or services be distributed?
   * Will they be distributed in a store, through mail order, on consignment, private parties, or on the Internet?
   * Will you introduce new distribution or delivery systems to increase sales, serve customers, or gain an advantage over the competition?

3. Industry/Trend Analysis
   * What is happening in your industry? Is it growing, stable, or declining? Is it a new industry or has it been around for awhile?
   * What do you believe the future holds for this industry?
   * Describe the industry in terms of overall sales in the US or worldwide.
   * Use quotes from trade journals or websites in the industry to show why this is a good industry to get into and start a business.
   * How easily can customers find alternatives inside or outside your industry?

4. Customers/Target Market Analysis
   * Who are your customers? What does a customer profile look like? How would you describe your ideal customer? Where does the person live? What are the person's age, gender, occupation, income level, education level, family composition, ethnicity and nationality?
   * When your ideal customer comes to your business, what need or want is that person looking to address?
   * What are the buying patterns of your ideal customers?
   * How often do they buy from your business? How large is each sales transaction? Do they buy on impulse or after careful consideration? Do they buy full-price items or seek discounts or sales?
   * When making buying decisions, what does your ideal customer value most? Cost? Quality? Features? Convenience? Reliability? Your reputation? Your unique expertise? Your after-sale support? Your product guarantee?
   * How many customers will your business have? How large is the market & what percentage do you expect to serve?
   * What information do you have that supports your decisions about your customers?
   * What is the growth potential for this business? What is your plan to handle growth?
   * What information do you have that supports your decisions about growth?
   * What area will you be serving? Is there a demand for your product(s) in that area? How do you know that?
   * You may want to provide some statistical data to support your target market analysis such as population growth, median household income for counties, etc.

5. Competition
- List 3 or more competitors and their locations (address) and their proximity to your business.
- What products and services do they provide, and what are they charging?
- Describe their strengths and weaknesses.
- Have any new competitors recently entered the market or have any competitors in your market area gone out of business recently?
- How difficult is it for new competitors to enter your market area?
- What is your competitive advantage- why will customers buy from you instead of the competition?

6. Pricing Policy for Products/Services
- What is your pricing philosophy? Does your business want to be the high-end price choice? Middle-of-the-pack? Low end?
- How did you determine your pricing strategy?
- How do your current (or planned prices) compare with those of your competition? If your prices are higher, do you offer extra value? If you prices are lower, what affects your lower price and can your pricing sustain profitabilty?
- Do you plan to offer special pricing to gain trial and acceptance? If so, what is your plan for increasing prices later?
- How often do you alter your prices or offer sales pricing?
- Do you allow bargaining?
- Selling Terms: cash only, checks (personal, business, or both) credit/debit cards, house accounts?
- When are payments due, before or after completion? Do you require a deposit on special order jobs or large quantity orders?
- Determine your profit margin. How does it compare to the competition and the industry in general?

7. Cost
- Describe your fixed expenses verses variable expenses. How much are your fixed expenses on a monthly basis?
- Fixed expenses are expenses that must be paid month to month that do not change. (Ex. rent, insurance, payroll, bookkeeping, etc.)
- Variable Expenses- Expenses that vary month to month. (Ex. advertising, inventory, travel expenses, etc.)
- What is your breakeven point? How many units or services will you have to perform a month to cover your fixed expenses?

8. Business Image and Customer Service
- Are you personally going to take all calls?
- How will complaints or service problems be handled?
- Will there be a return policy?
- If there is a return policy or unsatisfied service agreement, what are the guidelines?
- Will there be uniforms if you have an office or store?
- In general will there be a certain look for your business and/or employees? If so, have you thought about when you will implement this plan? As soon as you open your doors or 6 months down the road or once you hit a certain number.

9. Marketing and Sales Strategy

- Describe how your target market will know where you are located? For example, will you use:
  - Website or EBay account
  - Run ads in the local newspaper and possibly the Yellow Pages
  - Community Events
  - Discounts or gift certificates as incentives
- Will you be joining the Chamber for networking?
- Will you have a logo on your business cards?
- Describe how and where you will reach your target audience? Community Events? Chamber Events?
- List some low-cost but effective ways of reaching your target market. Go into detail with prices regarding your promotions.
- What is your promotional plan?

10. Marketing Goals
- What is your dream- where do you see the business going in the next 2 to 5 years?
- Example goals:
  - I want to start a successful business.
  - I want to expand my existing market share.
  - I want to add new products/services.
- What are your objectives for each of these goals? Why do you think they are realistic? How will they be measured, and when will they be achieved?
  - Example objectives:
- I want to have a 10% profit margin in 12 months.
- I will increase sales by 50% in 24 months.
- I want to develop one new product/service within 18 months.

III.   Operational Plan

1. Location
   * Where will you be operating your business? (Out of home, store front, Internet)
   * Is this a prime location?
   * Are there enough people that frequent or work in the area for the business to be recognized?
   * Why did you choose this location? Why is it desirable?

2. Operations
   * Will you be using any type of computer system, cash register, printer, copier, fax and/or credit card processing device?
   * Will you need supplies for the office/store? (fixtures, signs, desk, etc.)
   * Who will manage record keeping, finances, and inventory? How often will you do inventory checks if necessary?
   * What types of insurance will you need? Ex. Business Insurance, Auto Insurance, Workman's Compensation, etc.
   * Attach copies of bids or policies.
   * What licenses, permits or regulations will affect your business? Attach copies of licenses, permits, or regulatory forms.
   * Who will your accountant, lawyer, insurance agent, and other advisory team members be? Provide names and addresses.
   * Will you have to collect and pay sales tax, and if so, how much and for which entity (state or city)?

3. Employees
   * Will you hire employees or use subcontractors?
   * Who will handle what functions in the business? What are the qualifications or required skills you are looking for?
   * If you are hiring employees, how many will you hire and what will their duties be?
   * Who will hire, train, and supervise them? What will it cost the company the first two years?
   * What will your employee salaries or hourly rates be for the first two years?

4. Contingency Plan
   * What contingency plans have you made for you?
     - What will you do if you become sick or are injured, or in the event of a personal or family emergency that takes you away from the business? Who will take care of the business? How much will it cost?
     - What will you do if your car breaks down?
     - What will you do if your day-care provider can't take care of your child(ren) today, or if your child(ren) are too sick to go to school?
   * What contingency plans have you made for the business?
     - What will you do if sales are not what you expected?
   * What will you do to increase them?
     - What will you do if costs are higher than you expected?
   * What will you do to decrease them?
     - How will you make decisions to continue to stabilize or increase your cash flow and profits?
     - What will you do if your competitor lowers its prices?

IV.   Financial Plan

1. Describe the following:
   * How much of your own money will you be using to start the business and how much extra would you need to borrow? (See Start up Cost Sheet)
   * Provide an itemized detail of the loan request.
   * Include the supplier of the item or where the quote came from. If you have a written quote, please provide as supporting documents
   * Do you have any other means of income or will you be relying solely on the start-up business and its funds?
   * Can you do the business part time and have another job on the side especially for the first few months while the business is getting started?
   * What do you foresee the business making and expenses that it will incur in the 1st year? Attach Cash Flow Statement with detailed assumptions of income generated and expenses.
   * What do you anticipate the cash flow projections to look like for years two and three? Please provide a cash flow statement for the second and third years. (See Cash Flow Handout)

2. Discuss your credit
   * Do you have any of the following:
     o Bankruptcies, Judgments, Liens, Back Taxes, Late Payments, Child Support, Medical Bills - Please explain any that apply to you in detail.
     o Ex. The reason for the occurrence, if you have payment plans, what is that arrangement & is it current, if bankruptcy has been discharged then provide documentation

   * Have you pulled your credit in the last year?

3. Be prepared to fill out:
   * Loan application
   * Breakeven Analysis
   * Personal Budget Statement - Monthly Expenses
   * Personal Financial Statement
   * 12 month cash flow statement with a detailed assumption sheet describing how you came up with the income and expense projections. Be prepared to fill out second and third year projections. It is not necessary to provide detailed assumptions for years two and three.

V.   Supporting Documents

- Tax returns for the last 3 years (Business and/or Personal)
- Copy of license and other legal documents
- Copy of referrals
- 3 Business References (eg. Lawyer, Accountant, Supplier, Customer, or Professional Associates)
- 3 Personal References
- Copy of proposed lease or purchase agreement for building space
- Insurance declarations
- Floor plans, design layouts, etc.
- Sample brochures, business cards, or advertising material
- Letters of intent from suppliers (if necessary)
- If your business is already in existence you will need to provide 2 years of Profit & Loss (shown yearly or on a monthly basis).

HOW TO USE O.P.M.
(Other People's Money)

There are several alternative sources of funding outside of your own money to finance your business. Some include crowdfunding, loans, grants, and more. OPM provides large returns and creates a velocity of money. OPM is a type of good debt [which means any debt that puts money in your pocket.] Bad debt [Takes money out]. Using this strategy allows you to increase your ROI [Return on Investment] and helps you obtain more assets. So, instead of having $100,000 and putting 20% down for five properties, what if you use the OPM strategy and use the $100,000 to put 5% down on 20 properties? Hence, what I mean by saying is that the velocity of money helps you obtain more assets. A bank will lend about $80,000 for each property, which allows you to break your $100,000 down into $5,000 segments while using OPM to get the other $15,000 needed for each property at 5% interest. The loan payment would be $500 per month. Total returns on 20 properties under this strategy is $24,000 per year in cash flow, which would include rent from tenants, paying off loans and investors. After that, you refinance these properties [20], pay off any outstanding loans, and continue to receive cash flow from 20 properties.

OPM allows you to leverage other funds at maximum speed. Two other OPM strategies are private money and hard money. Private money is obtained from friends and family to form a financial partnership on a deal you buy. Hard money is when you use money from individuals or partnerships to earn a higher return on capital. Both OPM strategies give you leverage or borrowed capital.

So, in the context of the wealthy using other people's money to build their wealth. One thing the poor do all the time is set up a bank account and keep money in the bank. However, the bank has other plans, like lending out 95% of your money to wealthy and financially literate people through bank loans. The wealthy use loans [Other People's Money] to fund their ventures. Once the loan is repaid, they have a wealthy company worth millions or even billions. Another way they do this, and so should you, is by listing their companies, which grew to multi-million- and billion-dollar operations on the stock market/exchange. Once they have created a successful business, they look for other ways to recap their investment so that they can make a huge profit. By listing their company, ordinary people get to buy shares in the company. [OPM all the way across the board].

Now, residential real estate is nothing different; it is just another avenue the wealthy can use that you can also use. How? In this context, OPM is good because of the long-term loans to finance residential real estate construction. It also attracts a tax break that helps the wealthy gain more money. Banks are willing to give out mortgages. They only require an individual to fund a percentage of the cost of the house, and they will give you a mortgage that you can pay over a long period of time [i.e., several years].

The key point is that the money being borrowed [OPM] is paid over several years. This means you have the time to pay the loan using the rental money you get from the tenants. Rent pays the loan, and you will own the house. This is a simple strategy for you to consider and use. OPM is the greatest secret to wealth building.

SECTION 1202

Section 1202 is an opportunity for you to save millions in taxes. Section 1202 is a part of the Internal Revenue Code, which focuses on excluding capital gains taxation upon the sale of Qualified Small Business Stock [QSBS]. By qualifying under 1202, you are able to exclude up to $500 million in gains.

Under Section 1202, a noncorporate taxpayer may exclude [from gross income] 100% of the gain realized on the sale or exchange of QSBS acquired after September 27, 2010, and held for more than [5] five years. Your company must be deemed a small business when stock is issued. Nonetheless, you can grow to any magnitude, and the capital gains exclusion would still potentially apply.

Eligibility Requirements for 100% Exclusion

- The taxpayer received the stock at the original issue in exchange for money or property other than stock or as compensation for services to the corporation.

- The stock was issued after September 27, 2010, and must be held for at least five years.

- The issuer was a "qualified small business" when the stock was issued. A qualified small business is a business with aggregate gross assets not exceeding $50 million on a tax basis at the time or immediately after the stock is issued.

- The issuer must be engaged in a "qualified trade or business."

- The corporation meets an active business requirement "during substantially all of the taxpayer's holding period" for the stock. Also, the corporation's [C-Corp] stock may be held by a pass-through entity, which is common in private equity structures.

Other benefits include incentives for non-corporate taxpayers to invest in small businesses. The gain excluded under section 1202 is limited to a maximum of 10 million or ten times the adjusted basis of the stock.

- $\oplus$ Capital gains exemption from federal income tax on the sale of small business stock is the underlying purpose of this IRS Section.

- $\oplus$ 5 years before selling/portions of all realized gains excluded from federal tax.

⊕ American Recovery Reinvestment Act increased the exclusion rate from 50% to 75% for stocks purchased between February 18, 2009 – September 27, 2010.

⊕ Exempt from AMT [Alternative Maximum Tax] and the 3.8% NET Investment Income [NIT].

⊕ These businesses are prohibited, including financial service companies, hotels, law, engineering, architecture, brokerage services, and performing arts.

⊕ State taxes that conform to federal tax will also exclude capital gains. Example: $450,000 in taxable income, sell qualified small business tax bought on September 30, 2010, has a $30,000 profit. Taxpayers may exclude 100% of their capital gains.

Remember, the goal is to build a company, starting with your business credit first and then creating a revenue stream that will, in 5-6 years, put you in a position to complete a Section 1202 transaction. I'm not here to show you basic money ideas; if we are building wealth, you need to know all the secrets of the wealthy so that you can follow in their footsteps, then switch it up and push past them. Just because you're reading this thinking, how is this going to help me now? You are thinking too little; get the knowledge so you can be ready to capitalize down the road. Plan early so you don't miss out on these wealth-building strategies. Creating generational wealth is about the future, not now per se. Taking action now towards the future, not now per se. Taking action toward generational wealth will allow your kids, grandkids, and family to be set up to succeed and keep it going when you are long gone. Prison tends to capture our minds and lock them up to the point where we think we can't do much sitting in a cell; here is the knowledge that's unrestricted and written by a prisoner that has your best interest without even knowing you.

So, how do you set up your company under Section 1202 to avoid taxes? When is the company sold? You must first form your company as a C Corporation. The key here is that you can use a traditional C-Corp and set up an LLC; just make sure it's taxed as a C-Corporation. Do business for more than five years, then sell it, and there is no tax on the gain. That's all! It is really simple once you see the different sections of the tax code broken down this way. We habitually make it harder than it is in our minds. With the corporate tax rate at 21%, you can form a C-Corporation and only pay 21%; now, you can form a C-Corporation and only pay 21% on the income while paying no taxes on the gains from selling the company. So, this is a win-win situation when looking at the options of growing a company, then selling it, and not paying taxes on the sales/gains.

THE 401(K) RETIREMENT PLAN

Building wealth through a business also involves understanding the programs and services that you offer to your employees and yourself. Straight to the point: 401(k)s were not meant for or to be a retirement plan! They were designed and developed because, after the Great Depression, people weren't getting back into the stock market, so they created the 401(k) to make it easier for the average person to get into the stock market.

401l(k) refers to Section 401(k) of the IRS code, which allows employees to avoid taxation on parts of their income if they elect to receive it as deferred compensation rather than direct pay. So, a brief history:

- 1875 – First corporate pensions

- 1880 – First employee contribution plan

- 1935 – Social Security Established

- 1941-1945 – World War II spikes 5% boost in pensions

- 1978 – The Revenue Act of 1978 establishes 401(k) tax policies

- 2017 – 74% of companies of 401(k)

Before Congress enacted IRS Code Section 401{k), employers were given staff the option of receiving cash in lieu of an employer-paid contribution to their tax-qualified retirement plan accounts. Once Congress authorized IRS Code Section 401(k), it sent money straight to Wall Street. There are over 80 million people and over $7.3 Trillion in assets under management, representing 1/5 of the US retirement market. The United States government thought that enacting the Revenue Act of 1978 would somehow limit executives from having too much access to the perks of cash-deferred plans. 401(k) plans are a future version of "Pension Plans," which were introduced in 1875 by American Express. However, through the Great Depression and the Stock Market Crash of 1929, America's pension plans were tanking. Remember, when all financial history takes place that changes systems, there is a war. Show me the war; I will show you how the American Government changed financial policies that still hurt us today. Between 1929 and 1941, the Great Depression hit, and the US entered World War II in 1941. Financial and economic contractions were starting to bubble up. The Stock Market crashed in 1929, and the banking panics of 1930 had a lasting effect on things. World War II helped America out during the Great Depression because of military spending and supplies for the military, which meant that every person with an able body was called to work.

Pension plans were drying up once 401(k) entered the US in the 70s. Today, you might not know, but Pension Plans still exist. Social Security is technically a "Pension Plan" for the poor. This plan was created to help the poor in the 1930s who were starving to death, giving them money. By the 1960s, nearly half of the private sector pensions began to decline in the 1980s following a series of laws by Regan. This increased the volatility of pension funds from year to year by making annual contributions less predictable.

Some problems are high fees that can eat away at your savings growth, while you also have fees for investment in your account. Another problem is that 35% of the private sector employees don't have access to a 401(k) through their companies. Another 41% of millennials don't have a 401(k) through their jobs. Now, the wealthy have a "100-million-dollar 401(k) plan". You can do the same thing. The rich used retirement plans as tax shelters. This works because contributions are tax-deductible, but the investment earnings accumulate on a tax-deferred basis.

Another thing about 401(k) plans is that they are traditional, as the one mentioned above, and Roth 401(k) plans. Roth accounts, contributions, and withdrawals have no impact on income tax. The benefits of the Roth account are from tax-free capital gains. In 2006, employees have been allowed to designate contributions as a Roth 401(k) deferral. These contributions are made on an after-tax basis. For accumulated after-tax contributions and earnings in a designated Roth account [Roth 401(k)], "qualified distributions" can be made tax-free. There are benefits and problems with 401lk) plans; as a business owner, it's up to you to decide what's best for your employees and you.

7 Best 401(K) Plans

- ShareBuilder 401k
  - Setup: $45, $95 per month, or $1,140 annually
  - Employee Fees 0.83% of AVM
- Merrill Edge 401K Plan
  - Set-up: $390, $90 per month
  - Employee Fees: 0.52 of AVM, plus $4 per month
- Vanguard 401K Plan
  - Allows you to get access to Vanguards low-priced funds
- Fidelity Investment 401K Plans
  - Set-up: $500, $300 per quarter
- ADP 401K Plan
  - Set-up: Variable, $160 on standard plans
  - Employee Fees: 0.10% of covered assets

Pro se Tip: (!)

2022 Annual 401K Contribution limit is $20,500.

Remember the above is if you plan to offer 401K plans or if you plan to use them yourself. My opinion is that 401(k) plans border on the line of scam and stupid. Fees erode 50% to 70% of your potential retirement nest egg when it all boils down. Yes, they have the benefit of tax deferral, but as humans, we have this need for instant gratification that we don't look at the real reason behind tax deferral. Just a quick minute to touch on this so-called benefit. Why would anybody pay their taxes, not now, delay them, or defer them until they're ready to retire? You don't have anything to write off; you're paying higher taxes than ever. The IRS won't ask you to pay what your tax liability would have been if you'd been paying taxes all along. No! They will tell you to pay what your tax liability is at the time your taxes are due, which, let's be honest, when that time comes, you will pay a higher tax than if you pay it up into retirement. Scam or stupid, I'm stuck in the middle. On top of tax deferral being stupid, most are loaded up to 17 different fees and costs between the underlying investments and plan administrator.

Roth 401(k) can solve the tax deferral problem by allowing you to pay taxes today, deposit the after-tax amount, and never have to pay tax again. Not on growth or withdrawals! By checking the "Roth-eligible" box, you can pay tax today and let your growth and withdrawals be free from the IRS, but another option to think of is to use the money and put it in a life insurance policy to make compound interest. The wealthy turn life insurance policies into their own pension plans, and you can do the same.

The Simple 401(k) Plan

Yes, it's called that. My goal is to give you the information so you can make an informed decision for yourself and your business. Every financial field has pros and cons, but 401(k)s are now different.

Simple 401(k) plans are retirement savings accounts offered by business employers with 100 or fewer employees working like a 401(k), combining it with the simplicity of a **Simple IRA**. So, employees can defer some of their wages to the plan, and employers must either make a matching or nonelective contribution of a certain amount of each employee's wages. If you are eligible, as an employer, you can set up these plans with certain eligibility requirements, and the IRS sets limits on how much can be contributed each year.

- Must be at least 21 years old

- Have one year of service before they can participate

- Employees are allowed to borrow against balances

- Employees who provide SIMPLE 401(k) plans can't offer their employees any other options, and contribution limits are lower than those of traditional 401(k) plans.

- Geared towards the self-employed and small business owners

- You are able to structure your business in any form to qualify [i.e., LLC, Sole Proprietorship]

- Employees contribute with pre-tax dollars out of their paychecks, investing the fund in options provided by the plan administrator

- Employees can contribute a max of $14,000 in 2022. 50 and older can add an additional "catch-up" contribution of $3,000

- All employer contributions to a SIMPLE 401(k) are subject to an employer compensation cap. Which is $305,000 for 2022.

- All companies that offer this plan must file Form 5500 every year [see sample to follow]

Form 5500

Department of the Treasury
Internal Revenue Service

Department of Labor
Employee Benefits Security
Administration

Pension Benefit
Guaranty Corporation

Annual Return/Report of Employee Benefit Plan

This form is required to be filed under sections 104 and 4065 of the Employee
Retirement Income Security Act of 1974 (ERISA) and sections 6047(e),
6057(b), and 6058(a) of the Internal Revenue Code (the Code).

▶ **Complete all entries in accordance with
the instructions to the Form 5500.**

Official Use Only

OMB Nos. 1210-0110 / 1210-0089

2005

This Form is Open to
Public Inspection.

Part I Annual Report Identification Information

For the calendar plan year 2005
or fiscal plan year beginning   and ending

A This return/report is for:
(1) a multiemployer plan;
(2) a single-employer plan (other than a multiple-employer plan);
(3) a multiple-employer plan; or
(4) a DFE (specify)

B This return/report is:
(1) the first return/report filed for the plan;
(2) an amended return/report;
(3) the final return/report filed for the plan;
(4) a short plan year return/report (less than 12 months)

C If the plan is a collectively-bargained plan, check here ....▶

D If filing under an extension of time or the DFVC program, check box and attach required information. (see instructions) ....▶

Part II Basic Plan Information -- enter all requested information

1a Name of plan

1b Three-digit plan number (PN) ▶   1c Effective date of plan

Caution: A penalty for the late or incomplete filing of this return/report will be assessed unless reasonable cause is established.

Under penalties of perjury and other penalties set forth in the instructions, I declare that I have examined this return/report, including accompanying schedules, statements and attachments, as well as the electronic version of this return/report if it is being filed electronically, and to the best of my knowledge and belief, it is true, correct and complete.

Signature of plan administrator

SIGN HERE ▶   Date

a Type or print name of individual signing as plan administrator

Signature of employer/plan sponsor/DFE

SIGN HERE ▶   Date

b Type or print name of individual signing as employer, plan sponsor or DFE

For Paperwork Reduction Act Notice and OMB Control Numbers, see the instructions for Form 5500.   Cat. No. 13500F   Form **5500** (2005)

0 1 0 5 A A 0 1 0 R

v4.2

126

Form 5500 (2006)   Page **2**

2a   Plan sponsor's name and address (employer, if for single-employer plan) (Address should include room or suite no.)

1)

2)   C / O

3)

4)   2b   Employer Identification Number (EIN)

5)

6)   2c   Sponsor's telephone
                                                number

7)   2d   Business code
                                                                                  (see instructions)

8)

9)

3a   Plan administrator's name and address (if same as plan sponsor, enter "Same")

1)

2)   C / O

3)

4)   3b   Administrator's EIN

5)

6)   3c   Administrator's telephone number

7)

4   If the name and/or EIN of the plan sponsor has changed since the last return/report filed for this plan, enter the name, EIN, and the plan
     number from the last return/report below:

a   Sponsor's name

b   EIN   c   PN

Form 5500 (2005)   Page **3**

5   Preparer information (optional)

a   Name (including firm name, if applicable) and address

1)

2)

3)   **b**   EIN

4)

5)   **c**   Telephone number

6)

6   Total number of participants at the beginning of the plan year ....

7   Number of participants as of the end of the plan year (welfare plans complete only lines **7a**, **7b**, **7c**, and **7d**)

   a   Active participants ....

   b   Retired or separated participants receiving benefits ....

   c   Other retired or separated participants entitled to future benefits ....

   d   Subtotal. Add lines **7a**, **7b**, and **7c** ....

   e   Deceased participants whose beneficiaries are receiving or are entitled to receive benefits ....

   f   Total. Add lines **7d** and **7e** ....

   g   Number of participants with account balances as of the end of the plan year (only defined contribution plans complete this item) ....

   h   Number of participants that terminated employment during the plan year with accrued benefits that were less than 100% vested ....

   i   If any participant(s) separated from service with a deferred vested benefit, enter the number of separated participants required to be reported on a Schedule SSA (Form 5500) ....

0 1 0 5 A A 0 3 0 T

Form 5500 (2005)   Page 4

8   Benefits provided under the plan (complete **8a** and **8b** as applicable)

a   Pension benefits   (check this box if the plan provides pension benefits and enter below the applicable pension feature codes from the List of Plan Characteristics Codes printed in the instructions):

b   Welfare benefits   (check this box if the plan provides welfare benefits and enter below the applicable welfare feature codes from the List of Plan Characteristics Codes printed in the instructions)

9a Plan funding arrangement (check all that apply)   9b Plan benefit arrangement (check all that apply)

(1)   Insurance   (1)   Insurance

(2)   Code section 412(i) insurance contracts   (2)   Code section 412(i) insurance contracts

(3)   Trust   (3)   Trust

(4)   General assets of the sponsor   (4)   General assets of the sponsor

10 Schedules attached (Check all applicable boxes and, where indicated, enter the number attached. See instructions.)

a Pension Benefit Schedule   b Financial Schedules

1)   R   (Retirement Plan Information)   1)   H   (Financial Information)

2)   B   (Actuarial Information)   2)   I   (Financial Information–Small Plan)

3)   E   (ESOP Annual Information)   3)   A   (Insurance Information)

4)   SSA (Separated Vested   4)   C   (Service Provider Information)
                  Participant Information)
                                                        5)   D   (DFE/Participating Plan
                                                                        Information)

                                                        6)   G   (Financial Transaction Schedules)

                                                        7)   P   (Trust Fiduciary Information)

The bottom Line is that 401(k)s, Roth 401(k)s, SIMPLE 401(k) Plans, etc., have pros and cons. The history and different options are provided here for your review. The decision is up to you as to what way you choose.

BUSINESS IDEAS
(PASSIVE INCOME)

Passive income is highly sought after and often misunderstood. Its money is generated from investments. Passive income streams require an upfront investment and a lot of nurturing in the beginning. Some passive income ideas include:

- **Print on Demand**: Using Printify.com

- **Niche Content Blog**: Using Bluehost.com/Squarespace.com blogs that centered around a specific category.

- **Dropshipping**: Become the middleman using Shopify.com

- **Print Custom Items**: Using teespring.com

- Instagram Influencer: Using gumroad.com

- **Wholesale Products**: Fiji Water—buy at wholesale from Fiji and sell for retail on Amazon. Open a Wholesale Account.

- **Vending Machines**: If you use Pepsi products, you can contact them and get a free machine. Use the VendSoft App to track inventory.

- **Recession Proof Businesses**: Buy a laundromat, car wash, etc., or even a storage facility, HVAC Business, RV Park

- **Amazon FBA**: Seller on Amazon website, merch by Amazon (design, upload, create product descriptions)

- **Rent out stuff you own**: This includes extra space/storage space in the home. On neighbor.com

- **Car Rented Out On**: Turo.com

- **Used Baby Equipment on**: babyequip.com

- **Swimming pool on**: swimply.com

- **Backyard On**: Homecamper.com

- **Rent Out Truck On**: Coop.com (Ryder Company)

- **Rent Out Box Trucks On**: Fetchtruck.com

- **Rent Out Pick-Up Trucks**: Fluidtruck.com

- **Buy Existing Blog On**: empireflippers.com

- **Blog Builder Service**: Niche website builders allow you to create blogs from scratch, write blogs, and load them. The cost is $700 for 10,000 words of content.

- **Real Estate as Passive Income**: Pocket Properties allows you to buy shares for as little as $10 a share. Buy, sell, and trade like stocks. You can buy shares and gain a larger ownership stake in the property. Basically, you are buying individual slices of homes.

- **Fundrise**: Crowdfunding Investment in commercial real estate

- **Ground Floor**: Start with as low as $10, with investments in apartments and duplexes

- **Diversify Fund**: Start out with a minimum of $500

- **Roofstock**: allows you to buy cashflow-positive single-family rentals online at www.roofstock.com

- **Farmland Purchases**: Farm Together and Acre Trader give you steady, consistent, plus everyone needs to eat.

- **CDs**: Sallie Mae Bank has a 14-month penalty-free CD that can earn you 3.3% APY. The amazing thing about these penalty-free CDs is that you can withdraw your money anytime without penalty. Min $1 deposit, no fees. www.savebetter.com/banks/sallie-mae/14-month-no-penalty

- **CD Ladder**: You divide savings into CDs with different maturities. Ex. Suppose you have $10,000 to invest, but you invest $2,000 in five different CDs ranging in maturity from one through five years

  - **1 Year CD** – 2.50%

  - **2 Year CD** – 2.90%

  - **3 Year CD** – 3.05%

  - **4 Year CD** – 3.10%

  - **5 Year CD** – 3.15%

  Get your outside network to visit www.cit.com and build the above example with Citibank because they offer one of the best CD products. Higher rates mixed with a penalty-free CD option. (APY 2.75%)

- **Investing**: M1 Finance offers passive income through its free investing platform, allowing you to build a portfolio and invest for free. www.m1.com

- **Loaning to Businesses**:

  - **Revenue Sharing Notes**: Mainvest (www.mainvest.com) allows you to invest in a business that agrees to share a percentage of its future revenue until its investors receive a return on their investment. You can start with as little as $100, and your principal and interest will be repaid over time.

  - **Lend to Businesses for Inventory**: Worthy (www.worthybonds.com) invests in bonds that yield 5% annually. They take your funds and lend them to small businesses. Get started with as little as $10.

- o **Peer to Peer Lending**: Loaning money to borrowers who typically didn't qualify for traditional loans. Peer Street (www.peerstreet.com) is one of the best lending platforms. These loans will be used for real estate. Lend your money and get back the principal and interest on that loan. Median return on cash flow is 4.1%

- o **Bluehost**: (www.bluehost.com) offers free domain name/hosting, starting at just $2.95 monthly. Pick a topic you are interested in sharing with the world and begin to write it.

- o **Cash Back App**: Dosh (www.dosh.com) works with 10,000 retailers. All you do is download the app or go to their website and start creating cash-back passive income.

The bottom line is that passive income is how rich people also continue to build wealth. Passive income is money you receive from investments, etc. Sometimes, it requires little investment, time, or effort. You can leverage your time and effort to create income streams when you don't have money. That's why they always use the saying "It takes money to make money"; it is a myth! Some broke-minded people thought that the saying was true. But to be honest with you, until you move your mindset from poverty, blaming others type of mindset to a wealthy mindset that's driven by knowledge of financial literacy, you will continue to believe that poverty, broke-minded saying. The wealthy sit back and continue to capitalize on your lack of financial knowledge. But it's not that the wealthy sit back and ask you to give them your money; they have financial knowledge that allows them to go to the bank and ask for your money through a loan. (More on this later). Now, you have the knowledge through this book to create multiple streams of income. Remember, passive income requires something upfront: Time or money, and it is not free!

EMPLOYEE VS. BUSINESS OWNER

Building wealth as an employee works for CEOs like Elon Musk because they have $1 salaries with 70% equity in a company like Tesla and Space X. On the other hand, you can't accomplish this until you own a company or receive equity in the company on top of being a 9 to 5 salaried employee. Below you will see a diagram that shows the difference between an employee vs. a business owner and what separates them in the race to wealth: "when they are taxed"!

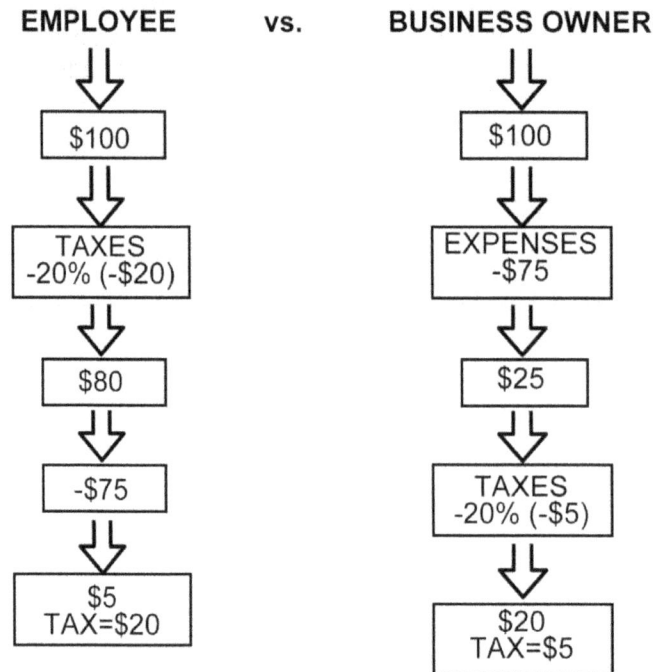

EMPLOYEE	vs.	BUSINESS OWNER
⬇⬇		⬇⬇
$100		$100
⬇⬇		⬇⬇
TAXES -20% (-$20)		EXPENSES -$75
⬇⬇		⬇⬇
$80		$25
⬇⬇		⬇⬇
-$75		TAXES -20% (-$5)
⬇⬇		⬇⬇
$5 TAX=$20		$20 TAX=$5

As the above diagram shows, employees are taxed 20% of the $100 first, thus taking $20. The business owner spends $75 on expenses, with $25 dollars of the original $100 left over, and at the same 20% tax as the employee, the business owner is left with $20 minus $5 for 20% taxes. The employee is always taxed first on their income, whereas the business is only taxed later on what is left over after expenses for the business. This is why building wealth through the formation of a business is always the right way to go. Get started now with building up your business and take control of your future while you sit in a prison cell or on your couch at home. "Plot, Plan & Execute."

BUSINESS FORMS INDEX

INDEX

- LLCs Articles of Organization
- LLC Sole Member Operating Agreement / Multi-Member
- Annual Report Form 1 "Filing Fee"
- Articles of Incorporation: Maryland & Delaware [C-Corp]
- TRADE NAME APPLICATION: "Maryland"

INSTRUCTIONS FOR DRAFTING
A LIMITED LIABILITY COMPANY

To create a Maryland Limited Liability Company (LLC) an originally executed **Articles of Organization** must be submitted to:
Department of Assessments and Taxation
301 W. Preston Street
Baltimore, MD 21201-2392

(1) Insert the name here. The name must not be misleadingly similar to that of another LLC, Corporation, Trade Name, Limited Partnership or Limited Liability Partnership on file with the Department and the name of the LLC must include one of the following:
a. Limited Liability Company
b. L.L.C.
c. LLC
d. L.C.
e. L C

(2) Insert the purpose of the LLC. A one or two sentence description of the business is sufficient.

(3) Insert the address of the LLC. The address must be in Maryland and **cannot be a P.O. box.**

(4) Insert the name and address **(cannot be a P.O. box)** of the resident agent. A resident agent is another entity or individual designated to accept service of process for the LLC. The resident agent can be any Maryland citizen who is over eighteen, a Maryland corporation or a Maryland LLC. This person must also sign the document.

(5) Execution - must be signed by any adult individual authorized by the persons forming the LLC.

(6) The resident agent must sign here.

(7) Insert the return address for any correspondence regarding this filing

NOTE: This list is the mandatory provisions. Any provision the parties decide is relevant may be added to the Articles of Organization. Documents must be **typed** or **printed**. No handwritten documents will be accepted.

FEES:
(1) Certificate of Organization $100.00
(2) Certified Copy of document above $20.00 + $1.00 page
(3) Certificate of Status at time of filing $20.00

Revised 8/04

ARTICLES OF ORGANIZATION

The undersigned, with the intention of creating a Maryland Limited Liability Company files the following Articles of Organization:

(1)   The name of the Limited Liability Company is:

_____

_____

(2)   The purpose for which the Limited Liability Company is filed is as follows:

_____

_____

(3)   The address of the Limited Liability Company in Maryland is _____

_____

(4)   The resident agent of the Limited Liability Company in Maryland is _____

whose address is _____

_____

(5) _____   (6) _____
                                                    Signature of Resident Agent

Signature(s) of Authorized Person(s)

Filing party's return address:

(7) _____

_____

MARYLAND STATE DEPARTMENT OF ASSESSMENTS & TAXATION   301 WEST PRESTON STREET BALTIMORE, MARYLAND 21201-2395

CHANGING Maryland *for the better*

SDAT, Articles of Organization (LLC)

Maryland State Department of Assessments & Taxation

NOTES: Due to the fact that the laws governing the formation and operation of business entities and the effectiveness of a UCC Financing Statement involves more than filing documents with our office, we suggest you consult an attorney, accountant or other professional. State Department of Assessments & Taxation staff cannot offer business counseling or legal advice.

Regarding annual documents to be filed with the Department of Assessments & Taxation. All domestic and foreign legal entities must submit a Personal Property Return to the Department. Failure to file a Personal Property Return will result in forfeiture of your right to conduct business in Maryland.

Where and how do I file my documents?
By mail or in-person submissions should directed to:
State Department of Assessments and Taxation, Charter Division
301 W. Preston Street; 8th Floor
Baltimore, MD 21201-2395

All checks must be made out to State Department of Assessments and Taxation. The cost to file documents should be included with the form. A schedule of filing fees is available online at http://dat.maryland.gov/businesses/Documents/FEES.pdf

Online business registration and document filing via the Maryland EGov Business portal. See the Maryland Business Express link on the homepage at www.dat.maryland.gov

The Department of Assessments and Taxation no longer accepts via facsimile (fax) corporate documents for filing or document copy request.

How long will it take to process my documents?
Regular document processing time is 4-6 weeks.

Expedited processing request will be handled within 7 business days. The expedited service fee is an additional $50.00 for each document; other fees may also apply.

Hand-delivered documents in limited quantities receive same day expedited service between 8:30 a.m. and 4:30 p.m., Monday through Friday. You must be in line no later than 4:15 p.m. in order to receive service that same day.

Online filed documents are considered expedited and will be processed within 7 business days.

Revised: August 2016

SOLE MEMBER OPERATING AGREEMENT
OF
_____, LLC

A Maryland Limited Liability Company

THIS OPERATING AGREEMENT ("Agreement") is made and entered into as of _____, 20____, by and among _____ LLC an Maryland Limited Liability Company (the "Company") and _____ executing this Agreement as the sole member of the Company (the "Member") and hereby states as follows:

NOW, THEREFORE, for good and valuable consideration the receipt and sufficiency of which is hereby acknowledged, it is agreed as follows:

1. Organization.

    1. Formation of LLC.

        The Member has formed a Maryland Limited Liability Company named _____, LLC by filing the Articles of Organization with the office in the State of Maryland on _____, 20____. The operation of the Company shall be governed by the terms of this Agreement and the applicable laws of the State of Maryland relating to the formation, operation and taxation of a LLC, specifically the provisions under Title 4A of the Maryland Code which set out the guidelines and procedures for the formation and operation of a LLC hereinafter collectively referred to as the "Statutes." To the extent permitted by the Statutes, the terms and provisions of this Agreement shall control in the event there is a conflict between the Statutes and this Agreement.

    2. Purposes and Powers.

        a) The purposes of the Company shall be:

            (i) _____; and

            (ii) To perform or engage in any and all activities and/or businesses for which limited liability companies may be engaged under the Statutes.

        b) The Company shall have all powers necessary and convenient to affect any purpose for which it is formed, including all powers granted by the Statutes.

    3. Duration.

The Company shall continue in existence until dissolved, liquidated or terminated in accordance with the provisions of this Agreement and, to the extent not otherwise superseded by this Agreement, the Statutes.

4. Registered Office and Resident Agent

The Registered Office and Resident Agent of the Company shall be as designated in the initial Articles of Organization/Certificate of Organization or any amendment thereof. The Registered Office and/or Resident Agent may be changed from time to time. Any such change shall be made in accordance with the Statutes, or, if different from the Statutes, in accordance with the provisions of this Agreement. If the Resident Agent shall ever resign, the Company shall promptly appoint a successor agent.

5. Capital Contributions and Distributions

The Member may make such capital contributions (each a "Capital Contribution") in such amounts and at such times as the Member shall determine. The Member shall not be obligated to make any Capital Contributions. The Member may take distributions of the capital from time to time in accordance with the limitations imposed by the Statutes.

6. Books, Records and Accounting

   a) Books and Records. The Company shall maintain complete and accurate books and records of the Company's business and affairs as required by the Statutes and such books and records shall be kept at the Company's Registered Office and shall in all respects be independent of the books, records and transactions of the Member.

   b) Fiscal Year; Accounting. The Company's fiscal year shall be the calendar year with an ending month of December.

7. Member's Capital Accounts

A Capital Account for the Member shall be maintained by the Company. The Member's Capital Account shall reflect the Member's capital contributions and increases for any net income or gain of the Company. The Member's Capital Account shall also reflect decreases for distributions made to the Member and the Member's share of any losses and deductions of the Company.

8. U.S. Federal / Maryland State Income Tax Treatment

The Member intends that the Company, as a single member LLC, shall be taxed as a sole proprietorship in accordance with the provisions of the Internal

Revenue Code. Any provisions herein that may cause the Company not to be taxed as a sole proprietorship shall be inoperative.

9   Rights, Powers and Obligations of Member.

   a.   Authority. _____, as sole member of the Company, has sole authority and power to act for or on behalf of the Company, to do any act that would be binding on the Company, or incur any expenditures on behalf of the Company.

   b.   Liability to Third Parties. The Member shall not be liable for the debts, obligations or liabilities of the Company, including under a judgment, decree or order of a court.

   c.   Rights, Powers and Obligations of Manager

   d.   The Company is organized as a "member-managed" limited liability company.

   e.   The Member is designated as the initial managing member.

   f.   Ownership of Company Property.

   The Company's assets shall be deemed owned by the Company as an entity, and the Member shall have no ownership interest in such assets or any portion thereof. Title to any or all such Company assets may be held in the name of the Company, one or more nominees or in "street name", as the Member may determine.

   g.   Other Activities.

   Except as limited by the Statutes, the Member may engage in other business ventures of any nature, including, without limitation by specification, the ownership of another business similar to that operated by the Company. The Company shall not have any right or interest in any such independent ventures or to the income and profits derived therefrom.

10. Limitation of Liability; Indemnification.

   a)   Limitation of Liability and Indemnification of Member.

      i.   The Member (including, for purposes of this Section, any estate, heir, personal representative, receiver, trustee, successor, assignee and/or transferee of the Member) shall not be liable, responsible or accountable, in damages or otherwise, to the Company or any other person for: (i) any act performed, or the omission to perform any act, within the scope of the power and authority conferred on the Member by this agreement and/or by the Statutes except by reason of acts or omissions found by a court of competent jurisdiction upon entry of a final judgment rendered and un-appealable or not timely appealed ("Judicially Determined") to constitute fraud, gross negligence, recklessness or intentional misconduct; (ii) the termination of the Company and this Agreement pursuant to the terms hereof; (iii) the performance by the Member of, or the omission by the Member to perform, any act which the Member reasonably believed to be consistent with the advice of attorneys, accountants or other professional advisers to the Company with respect to matters relating to the Company, including actions or omissions determined to constitute violations of law but which were not undertaken in bad faith; or (iv) the conduct of any person selected or engaged by the Member.

ii. The Company, its receivers, trustees, successors, assignees and/or transferees shall indemnify, defend and hold the Member harmless from and against any and all liabilities, damages, losses, costs and expenses of any nature whatsoever, known or unknown, liquidated or unliquidated, that are incurred by the Member (including amounts paid in satisfaction of judgments, in settlement of any action, suit, demand, investigation, claim or proceeding ("Claim"), as fines or penalties) and from and against all legal or other such costs as well as the expenses of investigating or defending against any Claim or threatened or anticipated Claim arising out of, connected with or relating to this Agreement, the Company or its business affairs in any way; provided, that the conduct of the Member which gave rise to the action against the Member is indemnifiable under the standards set forth in Section 10(a)(i).

iii. Upon application, the Member shall be entitled to receive advances to cover the costs of defending or settling any Claim or any threatened or anticipated Claim against the Member that may be subject to indemnification hereunder upon receipt by the Company of any undertaking by or on behalf of the Member to repay such advances to the Company, without interest, if the Member is Judicially Determined not to be entitled to indemnification.

iv. All rights of the Member to indemnification under this Section 10(a) shall (i) be cumulative of, and in addition to, any right to which the Member may be entitled to by contract or as a matter of law or equity, and (ii) survive the dissolution, liquidation or termination of the Company as well as the death, removal, incompetency or insolvency of the Member.

v. The termination of any Claim or threatened Claim against the Member by judgment, order, settlement or upon a plea of *nolo contendere* or its equivalent shall not, of itself, cause the Member not to be entitled to indemnification as provided herein unless and until Judicially Determined to not be so entitled.

11. Death, Disability, Dissolution.

a. Death of Member. Upon the death of the Member, the Company shall be dissolved. By separate written documentation, the Member shall designate and appoint the individual who will wind down the Company's business and transfer or distribute the Member's Interests and Capital Account as designated by the Member or as may otherwise be required by law.

b. Disability of Member. Upon the disability of a Member, the Member may continue to act as Manager hereunder or appoint a person to so serve until the Member's Interests and Capital Account of the Member have been transferred or distributed.

c. Dissolution. The Company shall dissolve and its affairs shall be wound up on the first to occur of:

   i. At a time, or upon the occurrence of an event specified in the Articles of Organization or this Agreement.

   ii. The determination by the Member that the Company shall be dissolved.

12. Miscellaneous Provisions.

a. Article Headings. The Article headings and numbers contained in this Agreement have been inserted only as a matter of convenience and for reference, and in no way shall be construed to define, limit or describe the scope or intent of any provision of this Agreement.

b. Entire Agreement. This Agreement constitutes the entire agreement between the Member and the Company. This Agreement supersedes any and all other agreements, either oral or written, between said parties with respect to the subject matter hereof.

c. Severability. The invalidity or unenforceability of any particular provision of this Agreement shall not affect the other provisions hereof, and this Agreement shall be construed in all respects as if such invalid or unenforceable provisions were omitted.

d. Amendment. This Agreement may be amended or revoked at any time by a written document executed by the Member.

e. Binding Effect. Subject to the provisions of this Agreement relating to transferability, this Agreement will be binding upon and shall inure to the benefit of the parties, and their respective distributees, heirs, successors and assigns.

f. Governing Law. This Agreement is being executed and delivered in the State of Maryland and shall be governed by, construed and enforced in accordance with the laws of the State of Maryland.

IN WITNESS WHEREOF, the Member has hereunto set such Member's hand as of the day and year first above written.

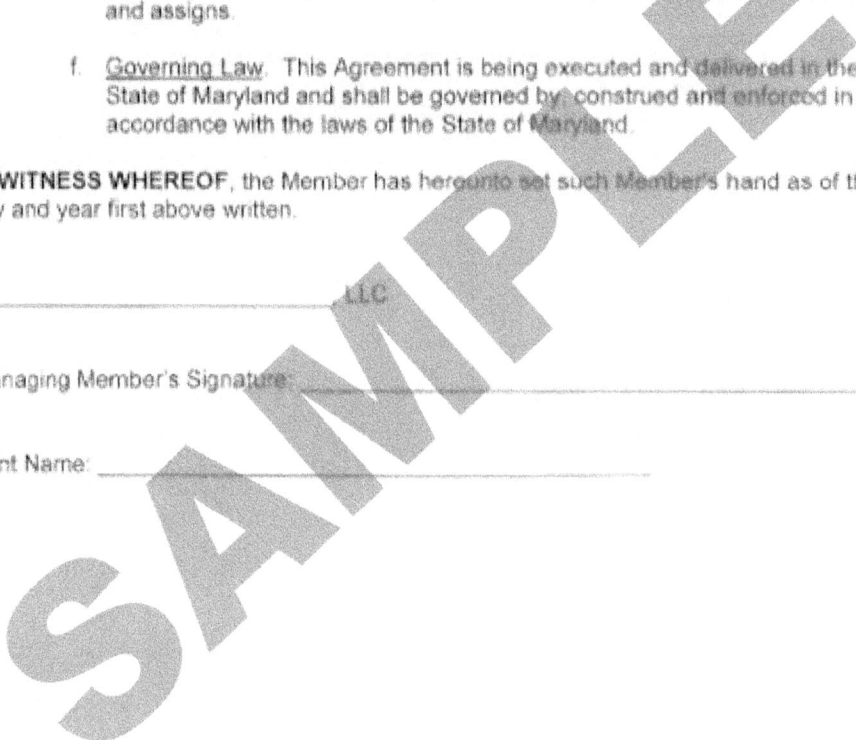

_____ LLC

Managing Member's Signature: _____

Print Name: _____

LIMITED LIABILITY COMPANY OPERATING AGREEMENT
OF
_____, LLC

FORMED IN THE STATE OF MARYLAND

1. Company Details

This Limited Liability Company Operating Agreement ("Agreement"), entered into on
_____, 20____ is a: (check one)

☐ - **Single-Member LLC**, entered into by _____, being the sole owner
with a mailing address of _____.

☐ - **Multi-Member LLC**, entered into by and between ____ Members known as:

Member #1: _____, with ownership of ____% of the Company, and a
mailing address of _____

Member #2: _____, with ownership of ____% of the Company, and a
mailing address of _____

Member #3: _____, with ownership of ____% of the Company, and a
mailing address of _____

Member #4: _____, with ownership of ____% of the Company, and a
mailing address of _____.

("Member(s)")

WHEREAS the Member(s) desire to create a limited liability company under the laws of
the State of Maryland ("State of Formation") and set forth the terms herein of the Company's
operation and the relationship any and all Member(s).

NOW, THEREFORE, in consideration of the mutual covenants set forth herein and
other valuable consideration, the receipt and sufficiency of which hereby are acknowledged,
the Member(s) and the Company agree as follows:

2. Name and Principal Place of Business

The name of the Company shall be _____, LLC with a principal place of
business located at _____, or at any other such
place of business that the Member(s) shall determine.

3. Formation

The Company was formed on _____, 20____ when the Member(s) filed the Articles of Organization with the office of the Secretary of State pursuant to the statutes governing limited liability companies in the State of Formation (the "Statutes").

4. **Member(s) Capital Contributions**

   a.) **Single Member Capital Contributions** (Applies ONLY if Single-Member): The Member(s) may make such capital contributions (each a "Capital Contribution") in such amounts and at such times as the Member(s) shall determine. The Member(s) shall not be obligated to make any Capital Contributions. The Member(s) may take distributions of the capital from time to time in accordance with the limitations imposed by the Statutes.

   b.) **Multi-Member** (Applies ONLY if Multi-Member): The Member(s) have contributed the following capital amounts to the Company as set forth below and are not obligated to make any additional capital contributions:

   Member #1: _____, with a capital contribution of: _____
   _____

   Member #2: _____, with a capital contribution of: _____
   _____

   Member #3: _____, with a capital contribution of: _____
   _____

   Member #4: _____, with a capital contribution of: _____
   _____

   Member(s) shall have no right to withdraw or reduce their contributions to the capital of the Company until the Company has been terminated unless otherwise set forth herein. Member(s) shall have no right to demand and receive any distribution from the Company in any form other than cash, and Member(s) shall not be entitled to interest on their capital contributions to the Company.

   The liability of any Member(s) for the losses, debts, liabilities, and obligations of the Company shall be limited to the amount of the capital contribution of the Member(s) plus any distributions paid to such Member(s), such Member(s)'s share of any undistributed assets of the Company; and (only to the extent as might be required by applicable law) any amounts previously distributed to such Member(s) by the Company.

5. **Management of the Company**

The Company's business and affairs shall be conducted and managed by the Member(s) in accordance with this Agreement and the laws of the State of the Formation.

   a.) **Single-Member** (Applies ONLY if Single-Member): The Member(s) of the Company has sole authority and power to act for or on behalf of the Company, to do any act that would be binding on the Company or incur any expenditures on behalf of the Company. The Member(s) shall not be liable for the debts, obligations, or liabilities of the

Company, including under a judgment, decree, or order of a court. The Company is organized as a "member-managed" limited liability company. The Member(s) is designated as the initial managing Member(s).

b.) **Multi-Member** (Applies ONLY if Multi-Member): Except as expressly provided elsewhere in this Agreement, all decisions respecting the management, operation, and control of the business and affairs of the Company and all determinations made in accordance with this Agreement shall be made by the affirmative vote or consent of Member(s) holding a majority of the Members' Percentage Interests.

Notwithstanding any other provision of this Agreement, the Member shall not, without the prior written consent of the unanimous vote or consent of the Member(s), sell, exchange, lease, assign or otherwise transfer all or substantially all of the assets of the Company; sell, exchange, lease (other than space leases in the ordinary course of business), assign or transfer the Company's assets; mortgage, pledge or encumber the Company's assets other than is expressly authorized by this Agreement; prepay, refinance, modify, extend or consolidate any existing mortgages or encumbrances; borrow money on behalf of the Company; lend any Company funds or other assets to any person or entity; establish any reserves for working capital repairs, replacements, improvements or any other purpose; confess a judgment against the Company; settle, compromise or release, discharge or pay any claim, demand or debt, including claims for insurance; approve a merger or consolidation of the Company with or into any other limited liability company, corporation, partnership or other entity; or change the nature or character of the business of the Company.

The Member(s) shall receive such sums for compensation as Member(s) of the Company as may be determined from time to time by the affirmative vote or consent of Member(s) holding a majority of the Member(s)' Percentage Interests.

6. Distributions

For purposes of this Agreement, "net profits" and "net losses" mean the profits or losses of the Company resulting from the conduct of the Company's business, after all expenses, including depreciation allowance, incurred in connection with the conduct of its business for which such expenses have been accounted.

The term "cash receipts" shall mean all cash receipts of the Company from whatever source derived, including without limitation capital contributions made by the Member(s)(s); the proceeds of any sale, exchange, condemnation or other disposition of all or any part of the assets of the Company; the proceeds of any loan to the Company; the proceeds of any mortgage or refinancing of any mortgage on all or any part of the assets of the Company; the proceeds of any insurance policy for fire or other casualty damage payable to the Company; and the proceeds from the liquidation of assets of the Company following termination.

The term "capital transactions" shall mean any of the following: the sale of all or any part of the assets of the Company; the refinancing of mortgages or other liabilities of the Company; the receipt of insurance proceeds; and any other receipts or proceeds are attributable to capital.

a.) **Single-Member** (Applies ONLY if Single-Member): A "Capital Account" for the Member(s) shall be maintained by the Company. The Member(s)'s Capital Account shall reflect the Member(s)'s capital contributions and increases for any net income or gain of the Company. The Member(s)'s Capital Account shall also reflect decreases for distributions made to the Member(s) and the Member(s)'s share of any losses and deductions of the Company.

b.) **Multi-Member** (Applies ONLY if Multi-Member): The "Capital Account" for each Member(s) shall mean the account created and maintained for the Member(s) in accordance with Section 704(b) of the Internal Revenue Code and Treasury Regulation Section 1.704-1(b)(2)(iv).

The term 'Members' Percentage Interests" shall mean the ownership percentage interests as mentioned in Section I of this Agreement.

During each fiscal year, the net profits and net losses of the Company (other than from capital transactions), and each item of income, gain, loss, deduction, or credit entering into the computation thereof, shall be credited or charged, as the case may be, to the capital accounts of each Member(s) in proportion to the Members' Percentage Interests. The net profits of the Company from capital transactions shall be allocated in the following order of priority: (a) to offset any negative balance in the capital accounts of the Member(s) in proportion to the amounts of the negative balance in their respective capital accounts, until all negative balances in the capital accounts have been eliminated; then (b) to the Member(s) in proportion to the Members' Percentage Interests. The net losses of the Company from capital transactions shall be allocated in the following order of priority: (a) to the extent that the balance in the capital accounts of any Member(s) are in excess of their original contributions, to such Member(s) in proportion to the excess balances until all such excess balances have been reduced to zero; then (b) to the Member(s) in proportion to the Members' Percentage Interests.

The cash receipts of the Company shall be applied in the following order of priority: (a) to the payment of interest or amortization on any mortgages on the assets of the Company, amounts due on debts and liabilities of the Company other than those due to any Member(s), costs of the construction of the improvements to the assets of the Company and operating expenses of the Company; (b) to the payment of interest and establishment of cash reserves determined by the Member(s) to be necessary or appropriate, including without limitation, reserves for the operation of the Company's business, construction, repairs, replacements, taxes and contingencies; and (d) to the repayment of any loans made to the Company by any Member(s). Thereafter, the cash receipts of the Company shall be distributed among the Member(s) as hereafter provided.

Except as otherwise provided in this Agreement or otherwise required by law, distributions of cash receipts of the Company, other than from capital transactions, shall be allocated among the Member(s) in proportion to the Members' Percentage Interests.

Except as otherwise provided in this Agreement or otherwise required by law, distributions of cash receipts from capital transactions shall be allocated in the following order of priority: (a) to the Member(s) in proportion to their respective capital accounts until each Member(s) has received cash distributions equal to any positive balance in their capital account; then (b) to the Member(s) in proportion to the Members' Percentage Interests.

It is the intention of the Member(s) that the allocations under this Agreement shall be deemed to have "substantial economic effect" within the meaning of Section 704 of the Internal Revenue Code and Treas. Reg. Section 1.704-1. Should the provisions of this Agreement be inconsistent with or in conflict with Section 704 of the Code or the Regulations thereunder, then Section 704 of the Code and the Regulations shall be deemed to override the contrary provisions thereof. If Section 704 of the Regulations at any time require that limited liability company operating agreements contain provisions which are not expressly set forth herein, such provisions shall be incorporated into this Agreement by reference and shall be deemed a part of this Agreement to the same extent as though they had been expressly set forth herein.

7. **Books, Records, and Tax Returns**

a.) **Single Member** (Applies ONLY if Single-Member): The Company shall maintain complete and accurate books and records of the Company's business and affairs as required by the Statutes, and such books and records shall be kept at the Company's Registered Office and shall in all respects be independent of the books, records, and transactions of the Member(s).

The Company's fiscal year shall be the calendar year with an ending month of December.

The Member(s) intends that the Company, as a Single-Member LLC, shall be taxed as a sole proprietorship in accordance with the provisions of the Internal Revenue Code. Any provisions herein that may cause the Company not to be taxed as a sole proprietorship shall be inoperative.

b.) **Multi-Member** (Applies ONLY if Multi-Member): The Member(s), or their designees, shall maintain complete and accurate records and books of the Company's transactions in accordance with generally accepted accounting principles.

The Company shall furnish the Member(s), within seventy-five (75) days after the end of each fiscal year, an annual report of the Company including a balance sheet, a profit and loss statement, a capital account statement; and the amount of such Member(s)'s share of the Company's income, gain, losses, deductions, and other relevant items for federal income tax purposes.

The Company shall prepare all Federal, State, and local income tax and information returns for the Company and shall cause such tax and information returns to be timely filed. Within seventy-five (75) days after the end of each fiscal year, the Company shall forward to each person who was a Member during the preceding fiscal year a true copy of the Company's information return filed with the Internal Revenue Service for the preceding fiscal year.

All elections required or permitted to be made by the Company under the Internal Revenue Code, and the designation of a tax matters partner pursuant to Section 6231(a)(7) of the Internal Revenue Code for all purposes permitted or required by the Code, shall be made by the Company by the affirmative vote or consent of Member(s) holding a majority of the Members' Percentage Interests.

Upon request, the Company shall furnish to each Member a current list of the names and addresses of all of the Member(s) of the Company, and any other persons or entities having any financial interest in the Company.

8. Dissolution and Liquidation

a.) **Single Member** (Applies ONLY if Single-Member): The Company shall dissolve and its affairs shall be wound up on the first to occur of (i) At a time, or upon the occurrence of an event specified in the Articles of Organization or this Agreement. (ii) The determination by the Member that the Company shall be dissolved.

Upon the death of the Member, the Company shall be dissolved. By separate written documentation, the Member shall designate and appoint the individual who will wind down the Company's business and transfer or distribute the Member's interests and Capital Account as designated by the Member or as may otherwise be required by law.

Upon the disability of a Member, the Member may continue to act as Manager hereunder or appoint a person to so serve until the Member's interests and Capital Account of the Member have been transferred or distributed.

b.) **Multi-Member** (Applies ONLY if Multi-Member): The Company shall terminate upon the occurrence of any of the following: (i) the election by the Member(s) to dissolve the Company made by the unanimous vote or consent of the Member(s); (ii) the occurrence of a Withdrawal Event with respect to a Member and the failure of the remaining Member(s) to elect to continue the business of the Company as provided for in this Agreement above; or (iii) any other event which pursuant to this Agreement, as the same may hereafter be amended, shall cause a termination of the Company.

The liquidation of the Company shall be conducted and supervised by a person designated for such purposes by the affirmative vote or consent of Member(s) holding a majority of the Members' Percentage Interests (the 'Liquidating Agent'). The Liquidating Agent hereby is authorized and empowered to execute any and all documents and to take any and all actions necessary or desirable to effectuate the dissolution and liquidation of the Company in accordance with this Agreement.

Promptly after the termination of the Company, the Liquidating Agent shall cause to be prepared and furnished to the Member(s) a statement setting forth the assets and liabilities of the Company as of the date of termination. The Liquidating Agent, to the extent practicable, shall liquidate the assets of the Company as promptly as possible, but in an orderly and businesslike manner so as not to involve undue sacrifice.

The proceeds of sale and all other assets of the Company shall be applied and distributed in the following order of priority: (1) to the payment of the expenses of liquidation and the debts and liabilities of the Company, other than debts and liabilities to Member(s); (2) to the payment of debts and liabilities to Member(s); (3) to the setting up of any reserves which the Liquidating Agent may deem necessary or desirable for any contingent or unforeseen liabilities or obligations of the Company, which reserves shall be paid over to a licensed attorney to hold in escrow for a period of two years for the purpose of payment of any liabilities and obligations, at the expiration of which period the balance of such reserves shall be distributed as provided: (4) to the Member(s) in proportion to their respective capital accounts until each Member has received cash distributions equal to any positive balance in their capital account, in accordance with the rules and requirements of Treas. Reg. Section 1.704-1(b)(2)(ii)(b); and (5) to the Member(s) in proportion to the Members' Percentage Interests.

The liquidation shall be complete within the period required by Treas. Reg. Section 1.704-1(b)(2)(ii)(b).

Upon compliance with the distribution plan, the Member(s) shall no longer be Member(s), and the Company shall execute, acknowledge and cause to be filed any documents or instruments as may be necessary or appropriate to evidence the dissolution and termination of the Company pursuant to the Statutes.

9. Purpose

The purpose of the Company is to engage in and conduct any and all lawful businesses, activities or functions, and to carry on any other lawful activities in connection with or incidental to the foregoing, as the Member(s) in their discretion shall determine.

10. Registered Office and Resident Agent

The Registered Office and Resident Agent of the Company shall be as designated in the initial Articles of Organization/Certificate of Organization or any amendment thereof. The Registered Office and/or Resident Agent may be changed from time to time. Any such change shall be made in accordance with the Statutes, or, if different from the Statutes, in accordance with the provisions of this Agreement. If the Resident Agent ever resigns, the Company shall promptly appoint a successor agent.

11. Term

The term of the Company shall be perpetual, commencing on the filing of the Articles of Organization of the Company, and continuing until terminated under the provisions set forth herein.

12. Bank Accounts

All funds of the Company shall be deposited in the Company's name in a bank account or accounts as chosen by the Member(s). Withdrawals from any bank accounts shall be made only in the regular course of business of the Company and shall be made upon such signature or signatures as the Member(s) from time to time may designate.

13. Miscellaneous

a.) **Meetings of Members** (Applies ONLY if Multi-Member): The annual meeting of the Member(s) shall be held on a day and month each year with at least thirty (30) days' notice given to the Member(s) prior to the meeting date which will be held at the principal office of the Company or at such other time and place as the Member(s) determine, for the purpose of transacting such business as may lawfully come before the meeting. If the day fixed for the annual meeting shall be a legal holiday, such meeting shall be held on the next succeeding business day.

The Member(s) may by resolution prescribe the time and place for the holding of regular meetings and may provide that the adoption of such resolution shall constitute notice of such regular meetings.

Special meetings of the Member(s), for any purpose or purposes, may be called by any Member.

Written or electronic notice stating the place, day, and hour of the meeting and, in the case of a special meeting, the purpose for which the meeting is called, shall be delivered not less than three (3) days before the date of the meeting, either personally or by mail, to each Member(s) of record entitled to vote at such meeting. When all the Member(s) of the Company are present at any meeting, or if those not present sign a written waiver of notice of such meeting, or subsequently ratify all the proceedings thereof, the transactions of such meeting shall be valid as if a meeting had been formally called and notice had been given.

At any meeting of the Member(s), the presence of Member(s) holding a majority of the Members' Percentage Interests, as determined from the books of the Company, represented in person or by proxy, shall constitute a quorum for the conduct of the general business of the Company. However, if any particular action by the Company shall require the vote or consent of some other number or percentage of Member(s) pursuant to this Agreement, a quorum for the purpose of taking such action shall require such other number or percentage of Member(s). If a quorum is not present, the meeting may be adjourned from time to time without further notice, and if a quorum is present at the adjourned meeting, any business matter may be transacted which might have been transacted at the meeting as originally notified. The Member(s) present at a duly organized meeting may continue to transact business until adjournment, notwithstanding the withdrawal of enough Member(s) to leave less a quorum.

At all meetings of the Member(s), a Member may vote by proxy executed in writing by the Member or by a duly authorized attorney-in-fact of the Member. Such proxy shall be filed with the Company before or at the time of the meeting.

A Member of the Company who is present at a meeting of the Member(s) at which action on any matter is taken shall be presumed to have assented to the action taken, unless the dissent of such Member shall be entered in the minutes of the meeting or unless such Member shall file a written dissent to such action with the person acting as the secretary of the meeting before the meeting's adjournment. Such right to dissent shall not apply to a Member who voted in favor of such action.

Unless otherwise provided by law, any action required to be taken at a meeting of the Member(s), or any other action which may be taken at a meeting of the Member(s), may be taken without a meeting if a consent in writing, setting forth the action so taken, shall be signed by all of the Member(s) entitled to vote with respect to the subject.

Member(s) of the Company may participate in any meeting of the Member(s) by means of conference telephone or similar communication if all persons participating in such meeting can hear one another for the entire discussion of the matters to be voted upon. Participation in a meeting pursuant to this paragraph shall constitute presence in person at such meeting.

b.) **Assignment of Interests** (Applies ONLY if Multi-Member): Except as otherwise provided in this Agreement, no Member or other person holding any interest in the Company may assign, pledge, hypothecate, transfer or otherwise dispose of all or any part of their interest in the Company, including without limitation, the capital, profits or distributions of the Company without the prior written consent of the other Member(s) in each instance.

The Member(s) agree that no Member may voluntarily withdraw from the Company without the unanimous vote or consent of the Member(s).

A Member may assign all or any part of such Member's interest in the allocations and distributions of the Company to any of the following (collectively the "permitted assignees"): any person, corporation, partnership or other entity as to which the Company has given consent to the assignment of such interest in the allocations and distributions of the Company by the affirmative vote or consent of Member(s) holding a majority of the Members' Percentage Interests. An assignment to a permitted assignee shall only entitle the permitted assignee to the allocations and distributions to which the assigned interest is entitled, unless such permitted assignee applies for admission to the Company and is admitted to the Company as a Member in accordance with this Agreement.

An assignment, pledge, hypothecation, transfer, or other disposition of all or any part of the interest of a Member in the Company or other person holding any interest in the Company in violation of the provisions hereof shall be null and void for all purposes.

No assignment, transfer, or other disposition of all or any part of the interest of any Member permitted under this Agreement shall be binding upon the Company unless and until a duly executed and acknowledged counterpart of such assignment or instrument of transfer, in form and substance satisfactory to the Company, has been delivered to the Company.

No assignment or other disposition of any interest of any Member may be made if such assignment or disposition, alone or when combined with other transactions, would result in the termination of the Company within the meaning of Section 708 of the Internal Revenue Code or under any other relevant section of the Code or any successor statute. No assignment or other disposition of any interest of any Member may be made without an opinion of counsel satisfactory to the Company that such assignment or disposition is subject to an effective registration under, or exempt from the registration requirements of, the applicable Federal and State securities laws. No interest in the Company may be assigned or given to any person below the age of 21 years or to a person who has been adjudged to be insane or incompetent.

Anything herein contained to the contrary, the Company shall be entitled to treat the record holder of the interest of a Member as the absolute owner thereof and shall incur no liability by reason of distributions made in good faith to such record holder, unless and until there has been delivered to the Company the assignment or other instrument of transfer and such other evidence as may be reasonably required by the Company to establish to the satisfaction of the Company that interest has been assigned or transferred in accordance with this Agreement.

c.) **Ownership of Company Property** (Applies ONLY if Multi-Member): The Company's assets shall be deemed owned by the Company as an entity, and the Member shall have no ownership interest in such assets or any portion thereof. Title to any or all such Company assets may be held in the name of the Company, one or more nominees or in "street name," as the Member may determine.

Except as limited by the Statutes, the Member may engage in other business ventures of any nature, including, without limitation by specification, the ownership of another business similar to that operated by the Company. The Company shall not have any right or interest in any such independent ventures or to the income and profits derived therefrom.

d.) **Right of First Refusal** (Applies ONLY if Multi-Member): If a Member desires to sell, transfer or otherwise dispose of all or any part of their interest in the Company, such Member (the "Selling Member") shall first offer to sell and convey such interest to the other Member(s) before selling, transferring, or otherwise disposing of such interest to any other person, corporation or other entity. Such offer shall be in writing, shall be given to every other Member, and shall set forth the interest to be sold, the purchase price to be paid, the date on which the closing is to take place (which date shall be not less than thirty nor more than sixty (60) days after the delivery of the offer), the location at which the closing is to take place, and all other material terms and conditions of the sale, transfer or other disposition.

Within fifteen (15) days after the delivery of said offer, the other Member(s) shall deliver to the Selling Member a written notice either accepting or rejecting the offer. Failure to deliver said notice within said fifteen (15) days conclusively shall be deemed a rejection of the offer. Any or all of the other Member(s) may elect to accept the offer, and if more than one of the other Member(s) elects to accept the offer, the interest being sold and the purchase price, therefore, shall be allocated among the Member(s) so accepting the offer in proportion to their Members' Percentage Interests, unless they otherwise agree in writing.

If any or all of the other Member(s) elect to accept the offer, then the closing of title shall be held in accordance with the offer, and the Selling Member shall deliver to the other Member(s) who have accepted the offer an assignment of the interest being sold by the Selling Member(s) and said other Member(s) shall pay the purchase price prescribed in the offer.

If no other Member(s) accepts the offer, or if the Member(s) who have accepted such offer default in their obligations to purchase the interest, then the Selling Member(s) within one-hundred and twenty (120) days after the delivery of the offer may sell such interest to any other person or entity at a purchase price which is not less than the purchase price prescribed in the offer and upon the terms and conditions which are substantially the same as the terms and conditions set forth in the offer, provided all other applicable requirements of this Agreement are complied with. An assignment of such interest to a person or entity who is not a Member(s) of the Company shall only entitle such person or entity to the allocations and distributions to which the assigned interest is entitled, unless such person or entity applies for admission to the Company and is admitted to the Company as a Member(s) in accordance with this Agreement.

If the Selling Member(s) does not sell such interest within said one-hundred and twenty (120) days, then the Selling Member(s) may not thereafter sell such interest without again offering such interest to the other Member(s) in accordance with this Agreement.

e.) **Admission of New Members** (Applies ONLY if Multi-Member): The Company may admit new Member(s) (or transferees of any interests of existing Member(s)) into the Company by the unanimous vote or consent of the Member(s).

As a condition to the admission of a new Member(s), such Member(s) shall execute and acknowledge such instruments, in form and substance satisfactory to the Company, as the Company may deem necessary or desirable to effectuate such admission and to confirm the agreement of such Member(s) to be bound by all of the terms, covenants, and conditions of this Agreement, as the same may have been amended. Such new Member(s) shall pay all reasonable expenses in connection with such admission, including without limitation, reasonable attorneys' fees and the cost of the preparation, filing or publication of any amendment to this Agreement or the Articles of Organization, which the Company may deem necessary or desirable in connection with such admission.

No new Member(s) shall be entitled to any retroactive allocation of income, losses, or expense deductions of the Company. The Company may make pro-rata allocations of income, losses, or expense deductions to a new Member(s) for that portion of the tax year in which the Member(s) was admitted in accordance with Section 706(d) of the Internal Revenue Code and regulations thereunder.

In no event shall a new Member(s) be admitted to the Company if such admission would be in violation of applicable Federal or State securities laws or would adversely affect the treatment of the Company as a partnership for income tax purposes.

f.) **Withdrawal Events** (Applies ONLY if Multi-Member): In the event of the death, retirement, withdrawal, expulsion, or dissolution of a Member(s), or an event of bankruptcy or insolvency, as hereinafter defined, with respect to a Member(s), or the occurrence of any other event which terminates the continued membership of a Member(s) in the Company pursuant to the Statutes (each of the foregoing being hereinafter referred to as a "Withdrawal Event"), the Company shall terminate sixty (60) days after notice to the Member(s) of such withdrawal Event unless the business of the Company is continued as hereinafter provided.

Notwithstanding a Withdrawal Event with respect to a Member(s), the Company shall not terminate, irrespective of applicable law, if within the aforesaid sixty-day period the remaining Member(s), by the unanimous vote or consent of the Member(s) (other than the Member(s) who caused the Withdrawal Event), shall elect to continue the business of the Company.

In the event of a Withdrawal Event with respect to a Member(s), any successor in interest to such Member(s) (including without limitation any executor, administrator, heir, committee, guardian, or other representative or successor) shall not become entitled to any rights or interests of such Member(s) in the Company, other than the allocations and distributions to which such Member(s) is entitled, unless such successor in interest is admitted as a Member(s) in accordance with this Agreement.

An "event of bankruptcy or insolvency" with respect to a Member(s) shall occur if such Member(s): (1) applies for or consents to the appointment of a receiver, trustee or liquidator of all or a substantial part of their assets; or (2) makes a general assignment for the benefit of creditors; or (3) is adjudicated a bankrupt or an insolvent; or (4) files a voluntary petition in bankruptcy or a petition or an answer seeking an arrangement with creditors or to take advantage of any bankruptcy, insolvency, readjustment of debt or similar law or statute, or an answer admitting the material allegations of a petition filed against them in any bankruptcy, insolvency, readjustment of debt or similar proceedings; or (5) takes any action for the purpose of effecting any of the foregoing; or (6) an order, judgment or decree shall be entered, with or without the application, approval or consent of such Member(s), by any court of competent jurisdiction, approving a petition for or appointing a receiver or trustee of all or a substantial part of the assets of such Member(s), and such order, judgment or decree shall be entered, with or without the application, approval or consent of such Member(s), by any court of competent jurisdiction, approving a petition for or appointing a receiver or trustee of all or a substantial part of the assets of such Member(s), and such order, judgment or decree shall continue unstayed and in effect for thirty (30) days.

g.) **Representations of Members** (Applies ONLY if Multi-Member): Each of the Member(s) represents, warrants and agrees that the Member(s) is acquiring the interest in the Company for the Member's own account for investment purposes only and not with a view to the sale or distribution thereof; the Member(s), if an individual, is over the age of 21; if the Member(s) is an organization, such organization is duly organized, validly existing and in good standing under the laws of its State of organization and that it has full power and authority to execute this Agreement and perform its obligations hereunder; the execution and performance of this Agreement by the Member(s) does not conflict with, and will not result in any breach of, any law or any order, writ, injunction or decree of any court or governmental authority against or which binds the Member(s), or of any agreement or instrument to which the Member(s) is a party; and the Member(s) shall not dispose of such interest or any part thereof in any manner which would constitute a violation of the Securities Act of 1933, the Rules and Regulations of the Securities and Exchange Commission, or any applicable laws, rules or regulations of any State or other governmental authorities, as the same may be amended.

h.) **Certificates Evidencing Membership** (Applies ONLY if Multi-Member): Every membership interest in the Company shall be evidenced by a Certificate of Membership issued by the Company. Each Certificate of Membership shall set forth the name of the Member(s) holding the membership interest and the Members' Percentage Interest held by the Member(s), and shall bear the following legend:

"The membership interest represented by this certificate is subject to, and may not be transferred except in accordance with, the provisions of the Operating Agreement of _____, LLC, dated effective as of _____, 20____ as the same from time to time may be amended, a copy of which is on file at the principal office of the Company."

i.) **Notices** (Applies ONLY if Multi-Member): All notices, demands, requests, or other communications which any of the parties to this Agreement may desire or be required to give hereunder shall be in writing and shall be deemed to have been properly given if sent by courier or by registered or certified mail, return receipt requested, with postage prepaid, addressed as follows: (a) if to the Company, at the principal place of business of the Company designated by the Company; and (b) if to any Member(s), to the address of said Member(s) first above written, or to such other address as may be designated by said Member(s) by notice to the Company and the other Member(s).

j.) **Arbitration** (Applies ONLY if Multi-Member): Any dispute, controversy, or claim arising out of or in connection with this Agreement or any breach or alleged breach hereof shall, upon the request of any party involved, be submitted to, and settled by, arbitration in the city in which the principal place of business of the Company is then located, pursuant to the commercial arbitration rules then in effect of the American Arbitration Association (or at any other time or place or under any other form of arbitration mutually acceptable to the parties involved). Any award rendered shall be final and conclusive upon the parties and a judgment thereon may be entered in a court of competent jurisdiction. The expenses of the arbitration shall be borne equally by the parties to the arbitration, provided that each party shall pay for and bear the cost of its own experts, evidence and attorneys' fees, except that in the discretion of the arbitrator, any award may include the attorney's fees of a party if the arbitrator expressly determines that the party against whom such award is entered has caused the dispute, controversy or claim to be submitted to arbitration as a dilatory tactic or in bad faith.

k.) **Amendments** (Applies ONLY if Multi-Member): This Agreement may not be altered, amended, changed, supplemented, waived, or modified in any respect or particular unless the same shall be in writing and agreed to by the affirmative vote or consent of Member(s) holding a majority of the Members' Percentage Interests. No amendment may be made to Articles that apply to the financial interest of the Member(s), except by the vote or consent of all of the Member(s). No amendment of any provision of this Agreement relating to the voting requirements of the Member(s) on any specific subject shall be made without the affirmative vote or consent of at least the number or percentage of Member(s) required to vote on such subject.

l.) **Indemnification** (Applies ONLY if Single-Member): The Member(s) (including, for purposes of this Section, any estate, heir, personal representative, receiver, trustee, successor, assignee and/or transferee of the Member(s)) shall not be liable, responsible or accountable, in damages or otherwise, to the Company or any other person for: (i) any act performed, or the omission to perform any act, within the scope of the power and authority conferred on the Member(s) by this Agreement and/or by the Statutes except by reason of acts or omissions found by a court of competent jurisdiction upon entry of a final judgment rendered and un-appealable or not timely appealed ("Judicially Determined") to constitute fraud, gross negligence, recklessness or intentional misconduct; (ii) the termination of the Company and this Agreement pursuant to the terms hereof; (iii) the performance by the Member(s) of, or the omission by the Member(s) to perform, any act which the Member(s) reasonably believed to be consistent with the advice of attorneys, accountants or other professional advisers to the Company with respect to matters relating to the Company, including actions or omissions determined to constitute violations of law but which were not undertaken in bad faith; or (iv) the conduct of any person selected or engaged by the Member(s).

The Company, its receivers, trustees, successors, assignees and/or transferees shall indemnify, defend and hold the Member(s) harmless from and against any and all liabilities, damages, losses, costs, and expenses of any nature whatsoever, known or unknown, liquidated or unliquidated, that are incurred by the Member(s) (including amounts paid in satisfaction of judgments, in settlement of any action, suit, demand, investigation, claim or proceeding ("Claim"), as fines or penalties) and from and against all legal or other such costs as well as the expenses of investigating or defending against any Claim or threatened or anticipated Claim arising out of, connected with or relating to this Agreement, the Company or its business affairs in any way; provided, that the conduct of the Member(s) which gave rise to the action against the Member(s) is indemnifiable under the standards set forth herein.
Upon application, the Member(s) shall be entitled to receive advances to cover the costs of defending or settling any Claim or any threatened or anticipated Claim against the Member(s) that may be subject to indemnification hereunder upon receipt by the Company of any undertaking by or on behalf of the Member(s) to repay such advances to the Company, without interest, if the Member(s) is Judicially Determined not to be entitled to indemnification as set forth herein.

All rights of the Member(s) to indemnification under this Agreement shall (i) be cumulative of, and in addition to, any right to which the Member(s) may be entitled to by contract or as a matter of law or equity, and (ii) survive the dissolution, liquidation or termination of the Company as well as the death, removal, incompetency or insolvency of the Member(s).

The termination of any Claim or threatened Claim against the Member(s) by judgment, order, settlement or upon a plea of *nolo contendere* or its equivalent shall not, of itself, cause the Member(s) not to be entitled to indemnification as provided herein unless and until Judicially Determined to not be so entitled.

14. Severability

This Agreement and the rights and liabilities of the parties hereunder shall be governed by and determined in accordance with the laws of the State of Formation. If any provision of this Agreement shall be invalid or unenforceable, such invalidity or unenforceability shall not affect the other provisions of this Agreement, which shall remain in full force and effect.

The captions in this Agreement are for convenience only and are not to be considered in construing this Agreement. All pronouns shall be deemed to be masculine, feminine, neuter, singular, or plural as the identity of the person or persons may require. References to a person or persons shall include partnerships, corporations, limited liability companies, unincorporated associations, trusts, estates, and other types of entities.

15. Entire Agreement

This Agreement and any amendments hereto may be executed in counterparts, all of which taken together shall constitute one agreement.

This Agreement sets forth the entire agreement of the parties hereto with respect to the subject matter hereof. It is the intention of the Member(s) that this Agreement shall be the sole agreement of the parties, and, except to the extent a provision of this Agreement provides for the incorporation of federal income tax rules or is expressly prohibited or ineffective under the Statutes, this Agreement shall govern even when inconsistent with, or different from, the provisions of any applicable law or rule. To the extent any provision of this Agreement is prohibited or otherwise ineffective under the Statutes, such provision shall be considered to be ineffective to the smallest degree possible in order to make this Agreement effective under the Statutes.

Subject to the limitations on transferability set forth above, this Agreement shall be binding upon and inure to the benefit of the parties hereto and to their respective heirs, executors, administrators, successors, and assigns.
No provision of this Agreement is intended to be for the benefit of or enforceable by any third party.

IN WITNESS WHEREOF, the parties hereto have executed and delivered this Agreement as of the date first above written.

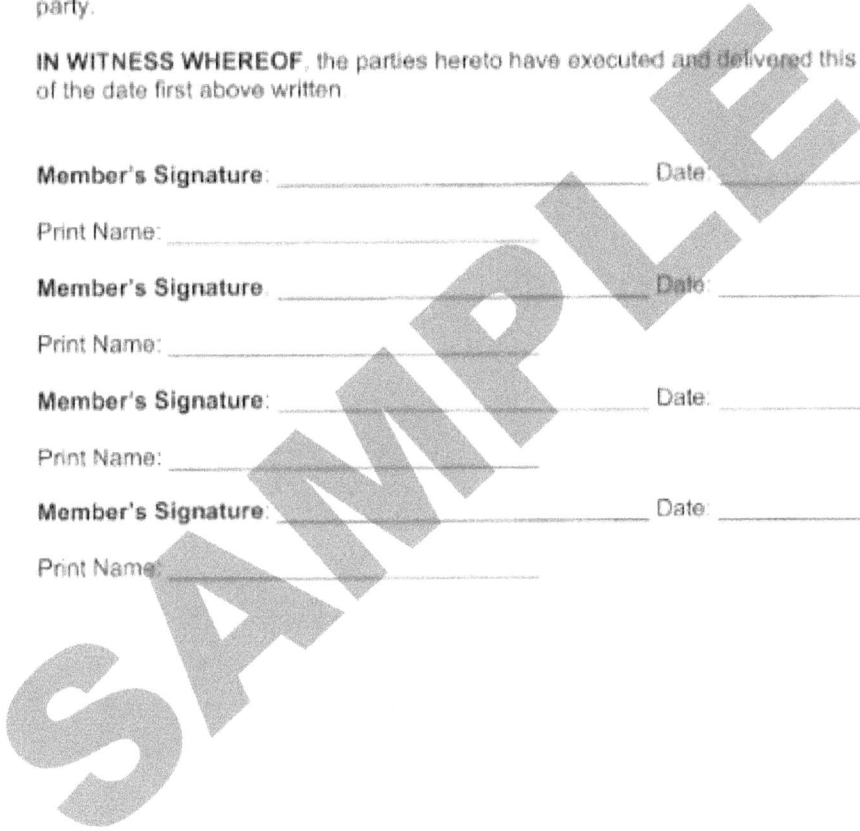

Member's Signature: _____ Date: _____

Print Name: _____

Member's Signature: _____ Date: _____

Print Name: _____

Member's Signature: _____ Date: _____

Print Name: _____

Member's Signature: _____ Date: _____

Print Name: _____

ANNUAL REPORT

MARYLAND STATE DEPARTMENT OF ASSESSMENTS AND TAXATION

Taxpayer Services - Charter Division P.O. Box 17052, BALTIMORE, MARYLAND 21297-1052

2020
Form 1
Due April 15th
Date Received
by Department

Type of Business Check one business type below	Dept. ID Prefix	Filing Fee		Type of Business Check one business type below	Dept. ID Prefix	Filing Fee
Domestic Stock Corporation	D	$300		Domestic Limited Liability Company	W	$300
Foreign Stock Corporation	F	$300		Foreign Limited Liability Company	Z	$300
Domestic Non-Stock Corporation	D	0		Domestic Limited Partnership	M	$300
Foreign Non-Stock Corporation	F	0		Foreign Limited Partnership	P	$300
Foreign Insurance Corporation	F	$300		Domestic Limited Liability Partnership	A	$300
Foreign Interstate Corporation	F	0		Foreign Limited Liability Partnership	S	$300
SDAT Certified Family Farm	A,D,M,W	$100		Domestic Statutory Trust	B	$300
Real Estate Investment Trust	D	$300		Foreign Statutory Trust	S	$300

SECTION I – ALL BUSINESS ENTITIES COMPLETE   ☐ PLEASE CHECK HERE IF THIS IS AN AMENDED REPORT

NAME OF BUSINESS

MAILING ADDRESS
☐ Check here if this is a change of mailing address

PLEASE NOTE This will not change your principal office address. You must file a Resolution to Change a Principal Office Address.

DEPARTMENT ID NUMBER
(Letter Prefix followed by 8 digits)

FEDERAL EMPLOYER IDENTIFICATION NUMBER
(9-digit number assigned by the IRS)

FEDERAL PRINCIPAL BUSINESS CODE
(If known, the 6-digit number on file with the IRS)

NATURE OF BUSINESS

TRADING AS NAME

EMAIL ADDRESS
Include an email to receive important reminders from the Department of Assessments and Taxation

SECTION II - ONLY CORPORATE ENTITIES COMPLETE
A. Corporate Officers (names and mailing addresses)

President_____

Vice President_____

Secretary_____

Treasurer_____

B. Directors (names only)

*Required Information for certain corporations, MD Code, Tax Property Article §11-101 - Please see instructions

*Total number of directors _____   *Total number of female directors _____

Department ID #_____

SECTION III – ALL BUSINESS ENTITIES COMPLETE

A. Does the business own, lease, or use personal property located in Maryland?   ☐ Yes ☐ No

If you answered **yes**, but your entity* is exempt, or has been granted an exemption from business personal property assessment by the Department, DO NOT complete the Personal Property Tax Return.

For religious groups, charitable or educational organizations, the form SD-1 is optional.

B. Does the business require or maintain a trader's (retail sales) or other license with a local unit of   ☐ Yes ☐ No
government?

Example: Clerk of the Court or Liquor Board

C. Did the business have gross sales in Maryland?   ☐ Yes ☐ No

If yes, $_____ total or amount of business transacted in MD.

D. Did the entity dispose, sell, or transfer ALL of its business personal property prior to January 1?   ☐ Yes ☐ No

If you answered yes, please complete form SD-1. Do not complete the Personal Property Tax Return.

If you answer "**Yes**" to questions A or B in Section III, and are not exempt as described in question A, please complete the Business Personal Property Tax Return (Form 1 Sections V through VII) and return it along with this Annual Report to the Department. The Personal Property Tax Return and important instructions can be found online at https://dat.maryland.gov/Pages/sdatforms.aspx#BPP

If you answer "**No**" to the questions A and B in Section III. above you DO NOT need to complete the Personal Property Tax Return. Please complete Section IV below, **sign** and return this Annual Report to the Department.

**Department of Assessments and Taxation, Charter Division
Box 17052, Baltimore, Maryland 21297-1052**

Questions? Contact Charter at 410-767-1340 • 888-246-5941 within Maryland • Email: sdat.charterhelp@maryland.gov

SECTION IV – ALL BUSINESS ENTITIES COMPLETE

By signing this form below, you declare, under the penalty of perjury, and pursuant to Tax-Property Article 1-201 of the Annotated Code of Maryland, that this Annual Report, including any accompanying forms, schedules, and/or statements, has been examined by you and, to the best of your knowledge and belief, is a true, correct, and complete Annual Report for the Entity listed in Section I.

A. Corporate Officer or Principal of Entity:

PRINT NAME_____

X SIGNATURE_____   DATE_____

MAILING ADDRESS_____

EMAIL ADDRESS_____   PHONE NUMBER_____

B. Firm or Individual, other than taxpayer, preparing this Annual Report/Personal Property Tax Return:

PRINT NAME_____

X SIGNATURE_____   DATE_____

MAILING ADDRESS_____

EMAIL ADDRESS_____   PHONE NUMBER_____

PLEASE BE SURE TO SIGN THIS ANNUAL REPORT TO AVOID REJECTION BY THE DEPARTMENT!

BUSINESS PERSONAL PROPERTY TAX RETURN
MARYLAND STATE DEPARTMENT OF ASSESSMENTS AND TAXATION, TAXPAYER SERVICES DIVISION
P.O. BOX 17052 Baltimore, Maryland 21297-1052; 410-767-1170 • 888-246-5941 within Maryland

2020
FORM 1
Due April 15th

Date Received
by Department

NOTE BEFORE FILLING OUT THIS PERSONAL PROPERTY RETURN MAKE CERTAIN YOU HAVE COMPLETED THE ANNUAL REPORT. A copy of the Annual Report form can be found online at https://dat.maryland.gov/Pages/sdatforms.aspx#BPP

SECTION V - ALL BUSINESS ENTITIES COMPLETE

NAME OF BUSINESS _____

MD DEPARTMENT ID NUMBER _____
(Letter prefix and 8 digits)*
*Required to ensure the correct Departmental account is credited

A. Mailing address _____

B. Email address _____

C. Is any business conducted in Maryland? [ ] Yes   [ ] No

D. Date began: _____

E. Nature of business _____

F. If business operates on a fiscal year: Start date_____ End date_____

G. Total Gross Sales, or amount of business transacted during prior year in Maryland $_____

If you report Total Gross Sales in question G of Section V, but do not report any personal property in Section VI, please explain how business is conducted without using personal property. If the business is using personal property of another business entity, please provide the name and address of that business entity below.

H. Explanation: _____

NAME OF THE OTHER BUSINESS _____

MD DEPT. ID OF THE OTHER BUSINESS _____

LOCATION OF THE OTHER BUSINESS _____

REMARKS

BUSINESS PERSONAL PROPERTY TAX RETURN OF DEPT ID# _____

2020
Form 1

SECTION VI - ALL BUSINESS ENTITIES COMPLETE

A. PROVIDE THE ACTUAL, PHYSICAL LOCATION OF ALL PERSONAL PROPERTY IN MARYLAND.

Show the exact physical location(s) of all personal property owned and used in the State of Maryland, including county, city or town, and street address (PO Boxes are not acceptable). This assures proper distribution of assessments. If property is located in two or more jurisdictions, provide a breakdown for each location by completing additional copies of Section VI (Pages 2 and 3 of Form 1). For 5 or more locations, please include the information per location in an electronic format (see Form 1 Instructions).

[ ] Check here if this is a change of location.

_____
Address, include City or Town, County and Zip Code

1. Please provide the original cost by year of acquisition for any furniture, fixtures, tools, machinery and/or equipment not used for manufacturing or research & development.

Year Acquired	A	B	C	D	E	F	G	Total Cost
2019	100							0
2018								0
2017								0
2016								0
2015								0
2014								0
2013								0
2012 & Prior								0
Totals	0	0	0	0	0	0	0	0

Describe property identified in B - G above: _____

2. Commercial Inventory – Furnish amounts from your most recent Maryland Income Tax Return.
Note: Businesses that need a Trader's License (Retail sales) must report commercial inventory here.

Average Monthly Inventory $ _____

    Opening Inventory date _____ Amount $ _____

    Closing Inventory date _____ Amount $ _____

3 Supplies Average Cost $ _____

4 Manufacturing and/or Research and Development (R&D) Avg. Monthly Inventory $ _____

BUSINESS PERSONAL PROPERTY RETURN OF DEPT ID# _____

	2020
	Form 1

5. Tools, machinery, and/or equipment used for manufacturing or research and development:
State the original cost of the property by year of acquisition. Include all fully depreciated property and property expensed under IRS rules. If this business is engaged in manufacturing / R&D, and is claiming such an exemption for the first time, a manufacturing / R&D exemption application must be submitted by September 1 or within 6 months after the date of the first assessment notice for the taxable year that includes the manufacturing / R&D property. Visit the website dat.maryland.gov for an application and additional information. If the property is located in a taxable jurisdiction, a detailed schedule by depreciation category should be included to take advantage of higher depreciation allowances.

Year Acquired	A	C	D	Year Acquired	A	C	D
2019				2015			
2018				2014			
2017				2013			
2016				2013 & prior			

Describe Property in C & D above: _____

Total Cost
$ 0

6. Vehicles with interchangeable Registration and/or Unregistered vehicles: (dealer, recycler, finance company, special mobile equipment, and transporter plates) and unregistered vehicles should be reported here. See specific instructions.

Year Acquired	Original Cost	Year Acquired	Original Cost
2019		2017	
2018		2016 & prior	

Total Cost
$ 0

7. Non-farming livestock:

Book Value $	Market Value $

8. Other personal property:
File separate schedule giving a description of property, original cost and the date of acquisition.

Total Cost
$

9. Property owned by others and used or held by the business or lessee or otherwise
File separate schedule showing names and addresses of owners, lease number, description of property, installation date and separate cost in each case.

Total Cost
$

10. Property owned by the business, used by others as lessee or otherwise.
File separate schedule showing names and addresses of lessees, lease number, description of property, installation date and original cost by year of acquisition for each location. Schedule should group leases by county where the property is located. Manufacturer lessors should submit the retail selling price of the property not the manufacturing cost. **For additional information regarding separate schedules please see Form 1 instructions at https://dat.maryland.gov**

Total Cost
$

BUSINESS PERSONAL PROPERTY RETURN OF DEPT ID# _____

**2020
Form 1**

SECTION VII - ALL BUSINESS ENTITIES COMPLETE

A. If this is the business' first Maryland personal property return, state whether or not it succeeds an established business and give name

_____

B. Does the business own any fully depreciated and/or expensed personal property located in Maryland? [ ] Yes [ ] No
   If yes, is that property reported on this return? [ ] Yes [ ] No

C. If the business transfers assets in or out of Maryland, or disposes of assets ($200,000 or more or 50% of the total property) during the prior year, complete Form SD-1. For additional details see Form 1 instructions at https://dat.maryland.gov

X Taxpayer's Signature/Date   Print Name   Phone Number & Email Address

X Preparer's Signature/Date   Phone Number & Email Address

Name and Address of Preparer

Mail the completed return to
DEPARTMENT OF ASSESSMENTS AND TAXATION
Personal Property Division
P.O. BOX 17052
Baltimore, Maryland 21297-1052

If you have questions contact the Personal Property Division
Telephone 410-767-1170
Toll free within Maryland 888-246-5941
Email: SDAT.PersProp@Maryland.gov

DEPRECIATION RATE CHART FOR PERSONAL PROPERTY

STANDARD DEPRECIATION RATE

Category A. 10% per annum
All property not specifically listed below

SPECIAL DEPRECIATION RATES
(The rates below apply only to the items specifically listed. Use Category A for other assets.)

Category B. 5% per annum*
Mainframe computers originally costing $500,000 or more

Category C. 20% per annum*
Autos (unlicensed), bowling alley equipment, brain scanners, carwash equipment, contractor's heavy equipment (tractors, bulldozers), fax machines, hotel, motel, hospital and nursing home furniture and fixtures (room and lobby), MRI equipment, mobile telephones, model home furnishings, music boxes, outdoor Christmas decorations, outdoor theatre equipment, photocopy equipment, radio and T.V. transmitting equipment, rental pagers, rental soda fountain equipment, self-service laundry equipment, stevedore equipment, theatre seats, trucks (unlicensed), vending machines, x-ray equipment

Category D. 30% per annum**
Data processing equipment and other computer based equipment, canned software

Category E. 33 1/3% per annum*
Blinds, carpets, drapes, shades. The following applies to equipment rental companies only: rental stereo and radio equipment, rental televisions, rental video cassette recorders and rental DVDs and video tapes

Category F. 50% per annum*
Pinball machines, rental tuxedos, rental uniforms, video games

Category G. 5% per annum*
Boats, ships, vessels, (over 100 feet)

Long-lived assets
Property determined by the Department to have an expected life in excess of 10 years at the time of acquisition shall be depreciated at an annual rate as determined by the Department

* Subject to a minimum assessment of 25% of the original cost
** Subject to a minimum assessment of 10% of the original cost

ARTICLES OF INCORPORATION
A Stock Corporation

In compliance with the requirements of the General Laws of the State of Maryland, and for the purposes of forming a for-profit business corporation in Maryland, the undersigned desire to form a corporation according to the following Articles of Incorporation.

Corporate Name

1. The name of the corporation is _____ (the "Corporation").

Purpose

2. _____

Duration

3. The duration of the Corporation is perpetual.

Registered Office and Registered Agent

4. The street address of the initial registered office is _____, _____ Maryland, _____. The name of the initial Registered Agent at this Registered Office is

_____

Street Address of the Principal Office

5. The street address of the principal office is _____, _____, Maryland, _____.

Initial Director

6. The initial board of directors will consist of one director (individually the "Director" and collectively the "Board of Directors"). The name of the person who is to serve as Director until the first annual meeting of stockholders or until their successors are elected and qualified is

_____

Name	Address	City	State	Zip Code
			Maryland	

Authorized Capital

7. The total number of shares of all classes of stock that the Corporation is authorized to issue is

   The aggregate par value of all the stock of all classes of stock is $0.00.

Class A Stock

8. The Corporation is authorized to issue a single class of stock. The total number of shares authorized is _____ par value shares of Class A stock and the par value of each of the authorized shares of Class A stock is $ US Dollars. This class of stock is entitled to receive the net assets of the Corporation on dissolution.

   The Class A voting, cumulative stock will have the following rights and privileges attached to them and be subject to the following conditions and limitations:

   a. The holders of Class A stock will be entitled to receive, as and when declared by the board of directors out of the monies of the Corporation properly applicable to the payment of dividends, cumulative, cash dividends, at the rate to be set by the board of directors.

   b. The Class A stock may from time to time be issued as a class without series or, may from time to time be issued in one or more series. If the Class A stock is issued in one or more series the board of directors may from time to time, by resolution before issuance, fix the number of stock in each series, determine the designation and fix the rights, privileges, restrictions, limitations and conditions attaching to the stock of each series but always subject to the limitations set out in the Articles of Incorporation.

   c. The holders of Class A stock will be entitled to one vote for each Class A stock held, and will be entitled to receive notice of and to attend all meetings of the stockholders of the Corporation.

   d. In the event of liquidation, dissolution, or winding up of the Corporation, the Class A stockholders will be entitled to share equally, share for share, in the distribution of the assets of the Corporation

Restrictions on Transfer

9. No shares of stock in the Corporation will be transferred without the approval of the board of directors of the Corporation either by a resolution of the board of directors passed at a board of directors meeting or by an instrument or instruments in writing signed by all of the board of directors.

Preemptive Rights

10. The stockholders of the Corporation have the preemptive right to purchase any new issue of stock in proportion to their current equity percentage. A stockholder may waive any preemptive right.

Amend or Repeal Bylaws

11. Bylaws may be adopted, amended, or repealed only with the approval of the board of directors.

Cumulative Voting

12. In an election of directors, each stockholder's number of votes will be calculated by multiplying the number of voting stock they are entitled to cast by the number of directors being elected. The stockholder may cast their total votes for a single director or may distribute them among two or more directors, as the stockholder sees fit.

Fiscal Year End

13. The fiscal year end of the Corporation is January 1st.

Indemnification of Officers, Directors, Employees and Agents

14. The board of directors, officers, employees and agents of the Corporation will be indemnified and held harmless by the Corporation and its stockholders from and against any and all claims of any nature, whatsoever, arising out of the individual's participation in the affairs of the Corporation. The board of directors, officers, employees and agents of the Corporation will not be entitled to indemnification under this section for liability arising out of gross negligence or willful misconduct of the individual or the breach by the individual of any provisions of this Agreement.

Limitation of Liability

15. The board of directors and officers of the Corporation will not be personally liable to the Corporation or its stockholders for any mistake or error in judgment or for any act or omission believed in good faith to be within the scope of authority conferred or implied by the Articles of Incorporation or by the Corporation. The board of directors and officers will be liable for any expenses or damages incurred by the Corporation or its stockholders resulting from any and all acts or omissions involving fraud or intentional wrongdoing.

Consent of Appointment by Resident Agent

16. Having been named as Resident Agent to accept service of process for the above named corporation at the place designated in this Articles of Incorporation, I am familiar with and accept the obligations of the appointment as Resident Agent and agree to act in this capacity.

Consenting Agent's Signature: _____
Printed Name: _____
Date: _____

Incorporator

17. The name and address of the incorporator of _____ are set out below.

Name	Address	City	State	Zip Code
			Maryland	

Execution

18. I, the undersigned, for the purpose of forming a corporation under the General Laws of the State of Maryland, do make, file and record this document, and do certify that I am 18 years old or older and the facts stated in this document are true, and I have accordingly set my hand to this document this _____ day of _____, A.D. 20_____.

BY:

_____ (Incorporator)

Filer Contact Information

19. In case of filing difficulties, please contact:

Name of Filer: _____

ARTICLES OF INCORPORATION
A Stock Corporation

In compliance with the requirements of the General Corporation Laws of Delaware, and for the purposes of forming a for-profit business corporation in Delaware, the undersigned desire to form a corporation according to the following Certificate of Incorporation.

Corporate Name

1. The name of the corporation is _____ (the "Corporation").

Purpose

2. _____

Duration

3. The duration of the Corporation is perpetual.

Registered Office and Registered Agent

4. The street address of the initial registered office is _____ Delaware, _____. The name of the initial Registered Agent at this Registered Office is _____ The county of the registered office is _____

Initial Director

5. The initial board of directors will consist of one director (individually the "Director" and collectively the "Board of Directors"). The name and address of the person who will serve as Director until the first annual meeting of stockholders or until successors are elected and qualified is set out below:

Name	Address	City	State	Zip Code
			Delaware	

Authorized Capital

6. The total number of shares of all classes of stock that the Corporation is authorized to issue is _____

Class A Stock

7. The Corporation is authorized to issue a single class of stock. The total number of shares authorized is _____ par value shares of Class A stock and the par value of each of the authorized shares of Class A stock is $ US Dollars. This class of stock is entitled to receive the net assets of the Corporation on dissolution.

The Class A voting, cumulative stock will have the following rights and privileges attached to them and be subject to the following conditions and limitations:

a. The holders of Class A stock will be entitled to receive, as and when declared by the Board of Directors out of the monies of the Corporation properly applicable to the payment of dividends, cumulative, cash dividends, at the rate to be set by the Board of Directors.

b. The Class A stock may from time to time be issued as a class without series or, may from time to time be issued in one or more series. If the Class A stock is issued in one or more series the Board of Directors may from time to time, by resolution before issuance, fix the number of stock in each series, determine the designation and fix the rights, privileges, restrictions, limitations and conditions attaching to the stock of each series but always subject to the limitations set out in the Certificate of Incorporation.

c. The holders of Class A stock will be entitled to one vote for each Class A stock held, and will be entitled to receive notice of and to attend all meetings of the stockholders of the Corporation.

d. In the event of liquidation, dissolution, or winding up of the Corporation, the Class A stockholders will be entitled to share equally, share for share, in the distribution of the assets of the Corporation.

Restrictions on Transfer

8. No shares of stock in the Corporation will be transferred without the approval of the Board of Directors of the Corporation either by a resolution of the Board of Directors passed at a Board of Directors meeting or by an instrument or instruments in writing signed by all of the Board of Directors.

Preemptive Rights

9.   The stockholders of the Corporation have the preemptive right to purchase any new issue of stock in proportion to their current equity percentage. A stockholder may waive any preemptive right.

Amend or Repeal Bylaws

10.   Bylaws may be adopted, amended, or repealed either by approval of the outstanding stock or by the approval of the Board of Directors. In adopting, amending or repealing a bylaw the stockholders may expressly provide that the Board of Directors may not adopt, amend or repeal that bylaw. The power of the Board of Directors is subordinate to the power of the stockholders to adopt, amend, or repeal bylaws.

Cumulative Voting

11.   In an election of Directors, each stockholder's number of votes will be calculated by multiplying the number of voting stock they are entitled to cast by the number of Directors being elected. The stockholder may cast their total votes for a single Director or may distribute them among two or more Directors, as the stockholder sees fit.

Fiscal Year End

12.   The fiscal year end of the Corporation is January 1st.

Indemnification of Officers, Directors, Employees and Agents

13.   The Board of Directors, officers, employees and agents of the Corporation will be indemnified and held harmless by the Corporation and its stockholders from and against any and all claims of any nature, whatsoever, arising out of the individual's participation in the affairs of the Corporation. The Board of Directors, officers, employees and agents of the Corporation will not be entitled to indemnification under this section for liability arising out of gross negligence or willful misconduct of the individual or the breach by the individual of any provisions of this Agreement.

Limitation of Liability

14.   The Board of Directors and officers of the Corporation will not be personally liable to the Corporation or its stockholders for any mistake or error in judgment or for any act or omission believed in good faith to be within the scope of authority conferred or implied by the Certificate of Incorporation or by the Corporation. The Board of Directors and officers will be liable for any

expenses or damages incurred by the Corporation or its stockholders resulting from any and all acts or omissions involving fraud or intentional wrongdoing.

Incorporator

15. The name and address of the incorporator of _____ are set out below.

Name	Address	City	State	Zip Code
			Delaware	

Execution

16. I, the undersigned, for the purpose of forming a corporation under the General Corporation Laws of Delaware, do make, file and record this document, and do certify that the facts stated in this document are true, and I have accordingly set my hand to this document this _____ day of _____, A.D. 20_____.

BY:

_____ (Incorporator)

Filer Contact Information

17. In case of filing difficulties, please contact:
    Name of Filer _____

Maryland State Department of Assessments & Taxation
TRADE NAME APPLICATION

FILING FEE: $25.00; EXPEDITED FEE: ADDITIONAL $50.00; TOTAL EXPEDITED SERVICE:
$75.00 (Make checks payable to Department of Assessments and Taxation)

Note: Prior to registering the business name of a home improvement company with the Department of Assessments & Taxation, an applicant is advised to contact the Home Improvement Commission at 410-230-6171 to ensure a specific name is available.

1) **TRADE NAME:** *Only one trade name may appear on this line)*

_____

2) **STREET ADDRESS(S) WHERE NAME IS USED:**

_____

CITY:_____ STATE:_____ ZIP:_____
Post office box number is only accepted when part of the physical address.

3) **FULL LEGAL NAME OF OWNER OF BUSINESS OR INDIVIDUAL USING THE TRADE NAME**

_____

If more than one owner, attach an additional sheet listing each owner with his/her address. Be sure each owner signs this form.

4) **THE SDAT ID OF THE ASSOCIATED BUSINESS IS:**

_____

(1 letter followed by 8 numbers – see item 4 of the Trade Name Application Instructions)

5) **ADDRESS OF OWNER**

CITY:_____ STATE:_____ ZIP:_____
Post office box number is only accepted when part of the physical address.

6) **DESCRIPTION OF BUSINESS**

_____

I affirm and acknowledge under penalties of perjury that the foregoing is true and correct to the best of my knowledge.

_____   _____
SIGNATURE OF OWNER (AUTHORIZED TITLE)   SIGNATURE OF OWNER (AUTHORIZED TITLE)

_____   _____
SIGNATURE OF OWNER(AUTHORIZED TITLE)   SIGNATURE OF OWNER (AUTHORIZEDTITLE)

301 West Preston Street-Room 801 -Baltimore, Maryland 21201
Phone (410) 767-1350 -TTY Users call Maryland Relay 1-800-735-2258 -Toll Free in MD 1-888-246-5941
Website: http://www.dat.maryland.gov

Rev 4/2022

MARYLAND STATE DEPARTMENT OF ASSESSMENTS & TAXATION   CHANGING Maryland for the Better   301 WEST PRESTON STREET, BALTIMORE, MARYLAND 21201-2395

Trade Name Application   (Revised: April 2022)   https://www.dat.maryland.gov

175

TRADE NAME APPLICATION INSTRUCTIONS

General Information
Registering this trade name will not guarantee acceptance by the Maryland Home Improvement Commission.
Prior to registering the business name of a home improvement company with the Maryland State Department of Assessments and Taxation, an applicant is advised to contact the Home Improvement Commission at 410-230-6171 to ensure a specific name is available.

1. The fee is $25.00. Checks should be payable to: **DEPARTMENT OF ASSESSMENTS AND TAXATION**

Filings submitted in hard copy may be hand delivered to drop boxes that SDAT maintains in the building lobby at 301 W. Preston Street, Baltimore, MD 21201. Please check the SDAT website for additional instructions regarding drop box submissions.

Mail the completed form and check to:

Charter Division
Department of Assessments and Taxation
301 W. Preston Street, Room 801 Baltimore,
Maryland 21201

2. For same day service the expedite fee is $425.00. Same day filings may be submitted online or hand delivered to the drop box by 10:00 am Monday-Friday. Fees must be paid by check or money order. No cash is accepted. Please visit our online business registration portal to register your trade name:
https://egov.maryland.gov/business express

3. Trade name applications must be signed to be accepted.

4. If the name is available and all items on the form are completed, SDAT will accept the filing for record and an acknowledgement, with the filing date will be sent to the "Address of Owner" (unless otherwise stated), ordinarily within 4 weeks of acceptance.

5. This filing is effective for five years from the date of acceptance by SDAT. During the last six months of the period the filing may be renewed for an additional five years. If not renewed, the Department will forfeit the trade name and a new application must be filed.

NOTICE: Acceptance of a trade name application does not confer on the owner any greater right to use the name than he otherwise already has. The Department checks the name only against other trade names filed with this Department. Federal trademarks, State service marks, records in other states and trade names are **not** meant to reserve the name for its owners, to act as a trademark filing or to confer on the owner any greater right to the name than he already possesses. For further information, contact your lawyer, accountant or financial advisor.

Revised: April 2022

HOW TO COMPLETE TRADE NAME APPLICATION

All blanks on the form must be typed or printed legibly, with black ink, with an original signature (no stamps, photocopies or carbon copy)
Numbers correspond to item numbers on the trade name application.

1. **TRADE NAME** – Only one trade name may appear on this line. To file more than one trade name, complete a separate application for each and send separate checks. **No trade name may contain a term that implies it is a type of entity that it is not (i.e., if the owner is an individual, "Inc." cannot be in the trade name).** Check the name on the business data search section of our web site – www.dat.maryland.gov.

2. **STREET ADDRESS(ES) WHERE NAME IS USED** – List the full address, including street address, city, state and zip code, Post office box number is only accepted when part of the physical address. Out-of-state addresses are acceptable.

3. **FULL NAME OF LEGAL ENTITY OR INDIVIDUAL USING THE TRADE NAME** – Legal entities may be owners of the trade name. If the legal entity is the owner the legal entity must be registered with MD Dept of Assessments and Taxation. If more than one owner, attach an additional sheet listing each owner with his/her address. Be sure each owner signs this form.

4. **SDAT ID OF THE ASSOCIATED BUSINESS** – Every Trade Name must be associated with a business which has been assigned an identification number by the MD Dept of Assessments and Taxation (a letter followed by 8 numbers). **Note:** All Unincorporated businesses that own or lease personal property (furniture, fixtures, tools, machinery, equipment, etc.) or anticipate owning or leasing personal property in the future, or need a business license must file an annual personal property return with this Department. Registration applications can be found at https://dat.maryland.gov/Pages/sdatforms.aspx.

5. **ADDRESS OF OWNER** – List the full address including street address, city, state and zip code. Post office box number is only accepted when a part of the physical address. Attach an additional sheet for all owners' addresses, if needed.

6. **DESCRIPTION OF BUSINESS** – State the nature of business.

7. **SIGNATURE** – Each person listed as an owner must sign. If a legal entity is the owner of the trade name, the person who signs for the entity must list his/her title.

Note: The laws governing the formation and operation of business entities involves more than filing documents with our office, we suggest you consult an attorney, accountant or other professional. The State Department of Assessments & Taxation staff cannot offer business counseling or legal advice.

Revised April 2022

ABOUT THE AUTHOR

C.A. Knuckles is currently incarcerated in Maryland. He has built Pro Se Prisoner into the go-to financial literacy publishing brand. This new book Pro Se Prisoner: Guide to Build Wealth, is the follow-up to his successful Pro se Prisoner: How to Buy Stocks and Bitcoin. Mr. Knuckles goal is to help prisoners build wealth and learn about finances, by giving them the knowledge to succeed while sitting in a prison cell. If you have questions or ideas or need advice about business-related matters, including investments, please contact him through his investment company.

The Attic Group, LLC

1 East Chase Street, Suite #1101

Baltimore, Maryland 21202

Mr. Knuckles would love to get your feedback about the book, make suggestions for the next one, or just let him know you liked it. Write to the above address. First, becoming wealthy requires changing your mindset, obtaining knowledge, and taking action! Thanks for becoming a Pro se Prisoner!

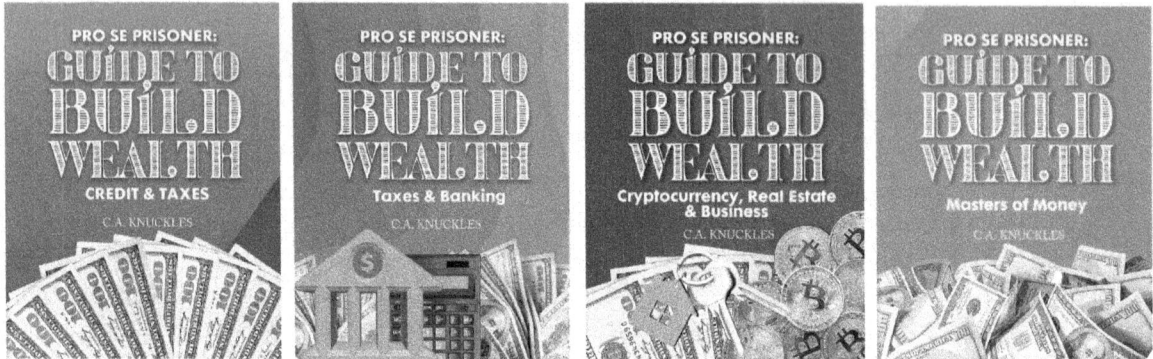

Transform your financial future and rehabilitation journey with this groundbreaking series designed for incarcerated individuals. Discover strategies to build credit, explore alternative investments, navigate taxes and banking, and delve into cryptocurrency and real estate, while unlocking your untapped wealth potential.

Book 1: "Pro se Prisoner: Guide to Build Wealth [Credit and Investing]
Build, fix, and obtain credit while incarcerated. Explore tailored investment opportunities.

Book 2: "Pro se Prisoner: Guide to Build Wealth [Taxes and Banking]
Leverage the tax code, use banking systems like billionaires, secure loans, and accelerate wealth-building.

Book 3: "Pro se Prisoner: Guide to Build Wealth [Cryptocurrency, Real Estate, and Business]
Dive into cryptocurrency, and build wealth through real estate, while setting up your business to maximize your business profitability.

Book 4: "Pro se Prisoner: Guide to Build Wealth [Masters of Money]
Practical strategies, tax insights, private equity knowledge, trust creation techniques, and credit management strategies.

Unlock credit, investing, taxes, banking, cryptocurrency, real estate, and business possibilities. Take charge of your financial future, even from behind bars. Get empowered today and become a Pro se Prisoner. Get your copy of the series now!

Only $29.99 Each
($20.99 plus $9 s/h incl. tracking)
SOFTCOVER, 8" x 10"

No Order Form Needed: Clearly write on paper & send with payment to:

Freebird Publishers 221 Pearl St., Ste. 541, North Dighton, MA 02764
Diane@FreebirdPublishers.com   www.Freebirdpublishers.com
We accept all forms of payment. Plus Venmo & CashApp!
Venmo: @FreebirdPublishers   CashApp: $FreebirdPublishers

FREEBIRD PUBLISHERS

We value our customers and would love to hear from you! Reviews are an important part in bringing you quality publications. We love hearing from our readers-rather it's good or bad (though we strive for the best)!

If you could take the time to review/rate any publication you've purchased with Freebird Publishers we would appreciate it!

If your loved one uses Amazon, have them post your review on the books you've read. This will help us tremendously, in providing future publications that are even more useful to our readers and growing our business.

Amazon works off of a 5 star rating system. When having your loved one rate us be sure to give them your chosen star number as well as a written review. Though written reviews aren't required, we truly appreciate hearing from you.

Sample Review Received on Inmate Shopper

poeticsunshine

★★★★★ **Truly a guide**
Reviewed in the United States on June 29, 2023
Verified Purchase

This book is a powerhouse of information. My son had to calm/ground himself to prioritize where to start.